"In *Seeking Out Goodn...* in the midst of darkn... This book is a call to a...

Dr. Heather Thompson Day, author of *It's Not Your Turn*

"Lately I've been wondering if it is possible to find unity among people who believe, think, and act differently from one another. And then I picked up Alex's book. *Seeking Out Goodness* offers a trail map to those of us who feel lost in the wilderness of cultural division. If there is any way forward, it is found here in these pages. It does not offer trite solutions but rather gospel-centered answers that come from authentic and thoughtful experience. Alex reminds us there is hope—for the church, for our communities, for our neighborhoods, and for the complexities found in our own homes. This book is just in time."

Krista Gilbert, home coach, author of *Reclaiming Home*, and cohost of *The Open Door Sisterhood* podcast

"Cynicism is the spirit of our age, but we will not be able to resist it passively. We need intentional steps for cultivating life where the world sows death, and Alexandra Kuykendall has provided it in these pages. With one eye on culture and the other on Scripture, this is a message for our moment!"

Sharon Hodde Miller, author of *Nice: Why We Love to Be Liked and How God Calls Us to Be More*

"As long as I can remember, Philippians 4:8 has been on repeat in my brain. A powerful and stirring verse, Alexandra Kuykendall calls it a 'road map for seeking out goodness.' Wow. Yes, please! I can't think of a better sister than Alex to lead us through this concept with love, humor, kindness, wisdom, and courage. As one who is blessed to call Alex friend, I can say she is the real deal. This book is part journey, part confession, part education, and a whole lot of opportunity for change. I found myself challenged to think about goodness more deeply, as well as to bring more of my issues, habits, and struggles straight to Jesus. Be prepared to be brought into truth through story, practical application, contemplation, and exercises that will yield beautiful change in you. Go big, friend, and dive into this book with the expectation of finding goodness!"

Kate Merrick, author of *Here, Now* and *And Still She Laughs*

"How do we not only understand this cultural moment we are living in but also learn to enter in to it? In *Seeking Out Goodness: Finding the True and Beautiful All around You* by Alexandra Kuykendall, you will find the answer! This is such a needed book that is full of thoughtful and practical wisdom to join God in what he is already doing in the world. 'The darkness is real,' writes Alexandra, 'But so is the light. And we know the light will overcome the darkness.'"

Patrick Schwenk, pastor, cohost of *Rootlike Faith* podcast, and author of *In a Boat in the Middle of a Lake*

"With the wisdom of a big sister and the heart of a trusted friend, Alex Kuykendall offers an invitation for readers to choose a different kind of path. It's a path marked by beauty and goodness, a path that runs toward the God who is the very definition of finding grace and mercy in the most unlikely of places. Given the topsy-turvy, upside-down world many of us find ourselves living in, *Seeking Out Goodness* is a necessary read for all of us today."

Cara Meredith, author of *The Color of Life*

"In a time of societal divisions and social media–fueled outrage, Alexandra Kuykendall's *Seeking Out Goodness* is a biblically rooted challenge to look for where God is at work in both the big and small moments of our lives."

Matthew Soerens, US Director of Church Mobilization
and Advocacy, World Relief

"*Seeking Out Goodness* is such a needed and timely book for exactly where we find ourselves in this current cultural moment. The principles found in these pages are timeless, but the examples and stories shared are relatable and helpful to followers of Jesus here and now. Alex Kuykendall is the real deal—living and modeling a life of integrity, truth, and beauty. The words penned on these pages bring together biblical truth, practical application, and refreshing encouragement for all those who find themselves weary in these challenging times."

Vivian Mabuni, speaker, podcast host, and founder
of Someday is Here; and author of *Open Hands, Willing Heart*

SEEKING OUT GOODNESS

Other Books
by Alexandra Kuykendall

The Artist's Daughter

Loving My Actual Life

Loving My Actual Christmas

Loving My Actual Neighbor

SEEKING OUT GOODNESS

GOODNESS

Finding the True and Beautiful All around You

ALEXANDRA KUYKENDALL

BakerBooks

a division of Baker Publishing Group
Grand Rapids, Michigan

Published by Baker Books
a division of Baker Publishing Group
PO Box 6287, Grand Rapids, MI 49516-6287
www.bakerbooks.com

Printed in the United States of America

Library of Congress Cataloging-in-Publication Data
Names: Kuykendall, Alexandra, author.
Title: Seeking out goodness : finding the true and beautiful all around you / Alexandra Kuykendall.
Description: Grand Rapids : Baker Books, a division of Baker Publishing Group, [2021]
Identifiers: LCCN 2021009307 | ISBN 9781540901378 (paperback) | ISBN 9781540901927 (casebound) | ISBN 9781493432882 (ebook)
Subjects: LCSH: God (Christianity)—Goodness.
Classification: LCC BT137 .K85 2021 | DDC 231/.4—dc23
LC record available at https://lccn.loc.gov/2021009307

To protect the privacy of those who have shared their stories with the author, some details and names have been changed.

The author is represented by the William K. Jensen Literary Agency.

Baker Publishing Group publications use paper produced from sustainable forestry practices and post-consumer waste whenever possible.

21 22 23 24 25 26 27   7 6 5 4 3 2 1

For Gabi, Genevieve,
Gracelynn, and Giulianna

You find what you're looking for.

CONTENTS

INTRODUCTION

you find what you're looking for

The morning's news headlines were a terrible welcome to a new day. CNN's home page flashed these bullet points, begging me to click and get more:

- A man fell to his death while taking pictures on a cliff in Arizona. Authorities discovered other remains while recovering his body.
- Man pleads guilty to aggravated murder of University of Utah student in exchange for life sentence.
- A Texas family sued to keep their baby on a ventilator. The hospital says the child is dead.
- A dangerous virtual cult is going global.

I closed my computer. Everything felt like bad news. Every headline brought more bleak information. Every Twitter take was tearing apart the opposite opinion. Every discussion

dripped with sarcasm and dismissal of any idea that dif-
fered. Politics. Pandemic. Economic divides. Racial tensions.
Violence near and far. *Surely the world hasn't shifted to a place
beyond hope,* I thought. *There must still be some good news for us
as people, some love to experience, some goodness to be found.*

A few minutes later as I scooped coffee grounds into
the pot's filter, I couldn't shake the thought that the world
is begging for good news. Jesus says, "Keep company with
me and you'll learn to live freely and lightly" (Matt. 11:30
MSG). On most days I do my darndest to follow Jesus, and
yet I am anything but light and free. It feels more like I
am dragging the world's despair. With each step the load
weighs heavier and my muscles are more fatigued, making
it difficult to stay motivated, to keep believing goodness
exists. Despite moments of overwhelm, I'm not ready to
give up looking, because though I know life is hard, I also
know it is beautiful.

I call myself a kitchen anthropologist because I stand
in my kitchen in Denver, Colorado, and observe the world
around me, trying to make sense of why people are doing
what they are and how that reflects on what they believe
about God and one another. This morning was no different
as I considered where God was still at work. Writing this
book is part of my kitchen anthropology. I hold no special
credentials other than a lot of observing and listening and
seeking out goodness in the middle of my ordinary days. I
think on questions like, *How is God moving in this situation?
Why do I think so? How are we, people who follow Jesus as Redeemer,
especially prepared to deal with this right now?*

I took my coffee back to my home office and looked
out the window to the beginning hints of a sunrise. Early

mornings are my time because that's when my house of
five other people is quiet and I can think. Out the window
I could see the sky changing—pink, orange, and blue in-
tensifying as the light got brighter. God was slowly turning
up the dimmer switch on the day. I saw the colors through
the branches and leaves of my neighbor's tree. The tree
and all its parts looked black against the orange and pink.
The contrast helped me notice both more easily. What I
noticed depended on what I chose to focus on. My gaze out
the window didn't change, but if I looked for the sunrise,
the tree became a frame for the vibrant color. If I focused
on the tree, the outline of the branches came into quick
clarity. I was looking at both simultaneously, but what I was
"seeking out" determined what I saw.

What We Know of God

This is a book about noticing. God's goodness is already
here. We don't have to pretend it up, talk it into existence,
or believe it to make it real. We know from Scripture that
God is good, and we know he is the same today as yesterday and will remain the same tomorrow. So his goodness
hasn't changed. We believe him to be a loving Creator who
makes all things new through his grace and redemption.
And because we know this about him, we can look for his
goodness in all places, and we can point to it when we find
it so that others can see it as well. We are meant to amplify
who he is. Think of holding up a magnifying glass to his
acts of love, his beautiful creation, his opportunities to love
him back and love others with refreshment, so that we can
remember that goodness is still here. "Every good gift and

every perfect gift is from above" (James 1:17 ESV), so every single good thing in this world can be traced back to him.

We remind ourselves and fellow Jesus followers of the truth so we can spur one another on to live out the great commandments of loving God and loving others. This in turn will remind others of the hope found in Christ. We are not that hope. He is the hope. Our job as kitchen, cubicle, classroom, hospital (or anyplace we find ourselves) anthropologists is to find echoes of his character and reflect them back to a world in need of good news. God's character—his love and mercy—is certainly good news.

If this feels a little woo-woo right now, hard to get your mind and hands around, this book is meant to make the process more concrete. Examples of what this has looked like for me and for others are mixed with practices to help you in your search so we can learn together what it means to seek out goodness. My hope is when you're done reading, you will have a better vision for what is good. It will jump out at you like the twists and turns of my neighbor's tree branches against the sunrise, because you have focused in on what you are looking for and can extract what is good.

Philippians 4:8 tells us where to center our thought life. This verse will act as our structure as we intentionally focus on finding goodness: "Finally, brothers and sisters, whatever is true, whatever is noble, whatever is right, whatever is pure, whatever is lovely, whatever is admirable—if anything is excellent or praiseworthy—think about such things." The promise follows in verse 9: "Whatever you have learned or received or heard from me, or seen in me—put it into practice. And the God of peace will be with you." Paul is telling his fellow Jesus followers to think on this list of goodness and then reflect those traits with our own actions. God will be with us in every part of the process.

As we use Philippians 4:8 as a road map for seeking out goodness, we will see how God demonstrates these qualities, how we are finding them around us, and how we can reflect them back to the larger world.

We Find What We're Looking For

If you're like me, the world feels exhausting right now. Everything has become controversial, a battleground for partisan fighting that reflects nothing of what God says he wants for people. On top of the intense cultural moment, each of us carries the stress of living our actual lives. Parents are sick, bills need to be paid, kids have to be educated and raised to be productive citizens. The amount of responsibility we each carry within a climate that feels toxic and combative is nothing short of overwhelming.

And yet we have good news. It's the good news that has followed humanity through every generational trial: God is with us. He has not changed. Though the political talking points, the community conflicts, and the pandemic devastation may have an intensity we haven't experienced before, he has. He has been with people through every human trial because he is, well . . . God. He is the Alpha and the Omega, the beginning and the end (Rev. 21:6), and he is not going anywhere. Though the ground we stand on feels unstable, he is unchanging and steady.

Because he does not change, we know his goodness remains here. If we are to survive the heaviness that fills our days, we must seek out what is good. The darkness is real.

But so is the light. And we know the light will overcome the darkness (John 1:5). So here is the million-dollar question: How? How do we seek out what is good when we feel paralyzed by what is difficult? How do we lift our heads enough? How do we make sure to hold on to the light in the midst of the darkness? That is what this book is about—how to search for, find, and recognize God's goodness.

A Prayer for
SEEKING

Lord, we know you make all things new.
You bring the sun up every day and the moon every
*   evening.*
You are dependable in your consistency
And surprising in your new growth.
Your goodness is both reliable and refreshing.

Open our eyes to where you are already at work.
Remind us with each discovery that you will not leave
*   us and you still have more to give.*
Help us to have new vision, a clarity that brings your
*   goodness to the front of our minds*
So that we may know more of you today, on this very
*   ordinary kind of day.*

Let us find you in the vacuuming, raking, and
*   scrubbing,*
In the wiping of tears, bottoms, and counters,
In the early morning light and midnight darkness,
In the typing, driving, walking, snoozing, baking of our
*   days,*
In the boredom, lovely, thrilling, and angst,
In the wild and wonderful, the bland and predictable.
In every part of our lives may we see evidence of who you
*   are.*

Holy Spirit, do a work in us so that we may reflect a teensy portion of God's goodness to our circles of people and creation on this planet.

Help us to reflect mercy,

Help us to offer grace,

Help us to be reconcilers,

Help us to be hope bearers,

So that those who are also seeking goodness will find your essence in us. May we not be barriers to your good news but amplifiers of it.

We trust you with this journey.

In Jesus and through Jesus we pray.

Amen.

QUESTIONS *for* REFLECTION

1. Where do you feel bad news most strongly? Where is there pain that overwhelms you? Is it old pain or new pain?

2. Do you believe there is goodness to be found? Why or why not?

3. What have you been seeking out? How is that reinforced by what you've found?

4. How have you seen good news? How does seeing it help you find more good news?

5. When considering what is true, noble, right, pure, lovely, admirable, excellent, or praiseworthy, what do you think will be the easiest for you to spot in the wild? What will be the most challenging?

Mining for the Gold

"Nonna's grandfather came from Ireland. You could focus on him."

Ten-year-old Gracelynn had just come home from school and was anxious to get started on her new assigned project: a report on a person from her family who had immigrated to the United States. My grandfather on my mother's side was the son of an Irish coal miner. He was the first person to come to mind.

"Okay, him."

Sometimes fourth graders are easy to please. And so we chose the mystery man we were labeling as "Nonna's grandfather," Gracelynn's great-great-grandfather. She was pleased. Now the first step was to find his name.

"William Hogan," my mom said when I called her. She said it with authority, so I was sure she was going to be a great resource on this assignment.

"Great. What else can you tell me?"

"He worked in the coal mines near Gunnison. He died when Dad was three years old. Dad was the youngest of ten."

Gunnison is a town on the other side of the Rocky Mountains from our home in Denver. It's a place where the city folk head to go white-water rafting or camping. The hint of Colorado's history is palpable, with ranches that still operate and a mountain valley where it's easy to imagine settlers looking around and deciding to stay.

My mom's knowledge of William Hogan stopped at the few pieces of information she gave me over the phone: his name and where he lived and his occupation at death. She knew her own father's name and birth date. I had a vague memory that she'd told me as a child that William had left a brother on the docks in Ireland. One brother was boarding a ship to the United States and the other was headed to Australia, both off on their respective adventures with no way of keeping in touch. No cell phones or emails, no forwarding addresses. As a child, I thought that story sounded slightly romantic and exciting. Now I hear desperation to make choices that would result in the grief of saying goodbye forever. It was time to do some research to find the details we needed for the project.

As any amateur genealogist would do, I went to the internet, a place where mining is required—a sifting through of what is untrue, unessential, and unimportant to find the gems I was looking for. I told Gracelynn I would help her find the facts, together we would make educated guesses about the details, and she could write out William's story.

We learned about coal mining in Colorado, the potato famine in Ireland, and travel to the New World. And then with all my internet scrolling, I found gold: A cemetery record in Gunnison, Colorado, that showed the birth and death years that lined up with my mother's memory. Then photos of a grave plot and shared tombstone for William and his wife, Sarah, my mother's namesake. Finally, the photo that made me gasp out loud as I realized what I'd discovered—the back of the tombstone had three engraved names with birth and death years. William and Sarah buried three of their children. Our search revealed that William Hogan's life was not only filled with the backbreaking work of climbing through the coal mines of our beautiful Rocky Mountains; it also contained the worst type of grief, losing a child, three times over. This final photo was not what I was looking for, but it gave me a whole new understanding of this man's experience in his "new world."

It wasn't lost on me as I clicked from site to site that we were mining for information about a miner. The process of mining is seeking out. It is often a toil to whittle away at what is unnecessary to discover what we're looking for. It isn't always the joy of the gold rush, the "cowabunga" of the big surprise; it is the disciplined step of looking for the next thing and the next thing. It is having eyes to see where God is at work, even if it doesn't seem obvious at first glance. It is finding treasure in the middle of what looks like a mountain of rock. It is venturing into unknown places, often dark and dangerous spots, to get what is valuable. It is separating what is good from what is not.

While my great-grandfather's mining work was difficult and sooty, it reminded me that the search for good can be hard. It is not meant for those who are looking for the easy, clean route. It is also the work of faith, because we must believe there is something worth seeking out if we are to go to all this trouble. We trust that there is a possibility that we will find treasure.

Part 1

the TRUTH,
the WHOLE TRUTH,
and NOTHING BUT
the TRUTH
(so help me, God)

I sat in the jury box trying to focus on the judge's opening instructions. I heard only snippets of his monologue. "A few days . . ." "No talking about the case . . ." "Breaks throughout the day . . ." I was too distracted by the thoughts of my four-year-old and nursing baby at my sister-in-law's for the day to give my full attention to the court-room happenings.

In the days that followed, my fellow jurors and I listened to expert witnesses with fancy credentials talk about medical protocols and medical records while technicians read phone message logs. We learned about kidneys . . . lots about kidneys. We watched the clock and covered our stomachs with our notebooks when we could feel ourselves getting hungry and our tummies started to grumble.

I'm kind of a natural juror. I like the thought of "experts." I enjoy hearing both sides of a story and then deciding where I stand on the question at hand. I also like the idea of getting to the bottom of something and finding the truth. I took notes, studied faces for emotion, and wondered when our next break would be so I could call my sister-in-law Lindsay to check in again.

The lawyers gave their closing arguments, and I walked into the jury room with confidence that this was a done deal. We could decide in ten minutes of deliberating, where we would just confirm to one another that this medical malpractice case was a big waste of our time and lots of resources. A good and easy "not guilty" verdict.

You know where this is headed. I was quick to learn that we didn't all see the evidence presented to us pointing to the same obvious result. Here we were, twelve jurors with twelve different life experiences, moral codes, and cultural filters to interpret the same information in front of us. We agreed on a forewoman to lead us through the process. The group discussion started with a respectful tone and was kicked off by a few brave souls volunteering to speak into the awkward silence. We felt the responsibility of our decision, and we all had our own versions of the nursing baby waiting for us at home. So we wanted to take our time to do right by both parties and also get out of there as quickly as possible.

The respectful tone faded, and I could hear strain and stress in people's voices. As it turns out, sifting through evidence to discern the truth can be hard.

Since the beginning of time, people have been searching for what is true. The pursuit of truth forms our cultures, informs our decisions, and shapes our understanding of how and why life exists. We can cover some pretty big questions in our search and have many sources to draw from. As Christians, we believe the Bible is God's inspired Word. It has authority. As does the Holy Spirit, who speaks directly to us and others. We are embodied souls, and our lived experiences reflect what is true of the world, the good and bad. Ultimately, we believe Jesus when he says, "I am the way and the truth and the life. No one comes to the Father except through me" (John 14:6). We turn to all these sources knowing they will enhance one another and reflect the same large story of the gospel with different hues and textures. In a world of "fake news," the foundations of our faith give us guideposts of truth as we walk through our days.

When searching for goodness, we are on the lookout for what is true (and what is not!). Philippians 4:8 starts right off with "Whatever is true." The problem is figuring out what exactly *is* true. We can't help but look at life through the lens of our personal experiences, which shape our biases, assumptions, and preconceived ideas. This is how we end up with animated jury deliberations. So we try to examine things from multiple angles to see if we're missing

27

something (the genius behind our peer jury system). We go back to the foundational truths of who God is and who we are in relationship to him. We keep our eyes open for truth because we want more of God, and we start with the truth that God is good.

The "not guilty" verdict I thought was so obvious turned out to be our decision in the end, but there was a lot of discussion to get us there. Agreeing on truth isn't automatic and almost always takes work.

We Don't Need to Be Afraid of the Truth

As a mother of four daughters, I've moderated a number of she-said, she-saids.

Girl 1: Mom, she _____ [hit me, looked at me mean, took a bite of my cereal].

Girl 2: I did NOT!

As details come out, I often find that someone's first version is not exactly the full story. The longer the partial-truth teller holds on to her unsubstantiated version, the more uncomfortable she gets because partial truth is unsatisfying, and hiding the truth takes a different kind of emotional work.

Let's pause here, right at the beginning of part 1, and decide we need to be honest during our search for goodness. If we believe God to be who he says he is—just, faithful, merciful, loving—then we can pursue truth with freedom. We don't need to pretend away or deny or hide from what is happening around us because God's character doesn't change. Will full honesty be comfortable? Not always. But our pursuit is for truth, not comfort.

If we trust God's character is unchanging, we can offer space for other people's questions and doubts because we know what is true will not change. We can also give ourselves permission to ask questions, seek reliable sources, and maintain curiosity as we learn more of the infinite God and how he operates in our finite world. We can hold to what we know is true and with humility loosely grasp the details that are still unknown. In this process we may find God's goodness in unexpected places because we've put preconceived ideas and presumptions aside and allowed God to show us his truth in new ways. We will offer others a more honest faith when we share where we have doubts.

To think on what is true sets our minds in the right place. It grounds us, keeping us away from things we fear or worry about that are not real. Much of our lives is spent considering, problem solving, and worrying about things that aren't even true. One of my daughters might cling to her version of a story because she is worried she'll get in trouble or will look silly if she is honest, but hiding from the truth is way more painful than any consequence had she just come clean and apologized. These distractions keep us from noticing, experiencing, and celebrating what God has for us that is true. Truth helps us find goodness.

The Truth Is Good

In church circles we often talk about balancing truth and grace. In this contrast the truth is usually presented as the harsh schoolmarm (reality), while grace is more like the grandma baking cookies (warm and soft and full of forgiveness and all). Truth is seen as the unfiltered photo with the gray roots and wrinkles, and grace is the filter that removes the unsavory. Truth becomes synonymous with confronting sin, perhaps throwing in some judgment and a dash of shame. In other words, truth is not fun. In this way it has gotten a bit of a bad rap, like somehow it is the bad news part of the Good News. But grace is also truth, and the Good News—God so loved the world that he came—is really good. We can reclaim truth to include good.

The world is a harsh place. We don't need to seek out that reality. The world is also full of beautiful moments and evidence of God's love. Both are true. The beautiful is no less true than the painful. Sometimes we like to play hierarchy of truth. Going back to the bad news part of the Good News, we assume the harsher the tone, the more true it must be. Uh-uh. In our everyday reclaiming of truth, we can look for the beautiful: a full pantry, dragonflies, babies who flail their legs when a sibling is in view, the sound of wind in the treetops, and a perfect flip of a cake out of its pan. All true. None harsh. All God's good gifts for today.

The good and the hard impact each other. They reverberate, changing each other's tone, shaping how we experience both, but the pain of this world doesn't negate the beauty, no matter how much we're told it does. In John 8:32, Jesus reminds the crowd outside the temple that following his teachings will be the key to freedom from their sins: "You will know the truth, and the truth will set you free." Jesus is the way, *the truth*, and the life, after all. It is knowing the truth about God and living from it that will move us from hurt, grief, and disappointment to see what is true and beautiful.

The Truth about God

It makes sense that we start with what we know to be true about God. He is kind of the main way we're going to find goodness. God's Word, which was inspired by him and written for all people in all times, is a good place to start. When I was talking with my friend Francie, she reminded me that we can filter things through God's metanarrative of creation, separation, reconciliation, and redemption. This is the larger story of God at work that is echoed throughout time and place. We see this pattern in humanity's larger story, but we also see it repeated over and over in our own stories. The micro reflects the macro. When looking for what is true and beautiful, I ask how a situation or circumstance fits into God's metanarrative. It helps me see what is true.

Scripture is God's living Word, meaning it can penetrate our spirits in a way that it wouldn't if it was just a bunch of old writing. We are meant to engage with it, meditate on it, *think on it.* It is the truth we can turn to over and over again that will point us toward hope. Scripture gives words to who God is. Here are a few things it tells us about God:

God is holy (Isa. 6:3).

God is love (1 John 4:8).

God is consistent and unchanging (Heb. 13:8).

God offers grace and mercy (Eph. 2:8–9).

God provides (Matt. 10:29).

PRACTICES FOR CONSIDERING GOD

Choose one of the descriptors of God listed on the previous page and do one or more of the following:

» Close your eyes and ask yourself what that word means to you.
» Pray the entire phrase as you breathe. Inhale: *God is.* Exhale: *loving.*
» Write the phrase out multiple times. Consider the words as you write them.

» Consider how this truth impacts your heart, your circumstances, and your upcoming decisions.
» Remember a time when you haven't known this to be true of God. Write how you felt.

» Look up the verse referenced and memorize it.

The Truth about You

You've likely played the game Two Truths and a Lie, where a person tells a group of people three things about himself or herself, and the group has to decide which of the three is the lie. From youth groups to office retreats, it's meant to be a funny way to get to know new details about one another. It is kind of fun to pull from what I know of someone to make an educated guess. It makes sense that a coworker would be a master gardener, given the floral prints she always wears. Not so likely she's been to all fifty states, given she hasn't taken a vacation in two years.

When it's my turn to share, I often freeze and give the worst possible (read: most obvious) answers:

1. I have four daughters.
2. I live in Denver.
3. Uhhhh . . . my cat was in the circus?

Not exactly nailing it.

Unlike my circus-cat answer, we can get really good at un-intentionally playing this game with the world, putting half-truths out for others to consume (see social media). So much so that we get our own lies and truths about ourselves mixed up and can't untangle them in our own minds. Things that have been said to us or done to us or just our human nature can distort the truth to the point that we forget who we are. We take in fake news, and it becomes part of the truth we believe. From the beginning of the human story, that snake in the garden has liked nothing more than for us to believe the untruths the world throws at us. From marketing campaigns that tell us our lives would be better if we only had a given product to our patterns of thinking that have narrowed in on our self-perceived shortcomings, we are constantly receiving messages about ourselves that are not true.

The human experience is about our relationship with God and the world he created. As the only creatures on earth made in his image, we are in a unique place to feel, think, experience, bond, grieve, and celebrate. It is not just due to natural selection that we are different from the rest of the life on this earth. It is our God-given identity that allows us to experience the complex, rich lives that we do. We are looking for God's goodness, and it is found in the truth of who we are. Remember that in the beginning when he created us, God called his creation good.

The creation part of the big story is that he made us and called us good. Here are a few reminders of who you are in the metanarrative, the redemption part of your story:

You are made in God's image (Gen. 1:26–27).

You are a sinner (Rom. 3:23).

You are a new creation (2 Cor. 5:17).

You are a citizen of heaven (Phil. 3:20).

You are loved (Col. 3:12).

You are chosen (1 Thess. 1:4).

You are set free (Gal. 5:1).

There is a reason we call the gospel the Good News. Our souls cheer when we hear its truth. We are desperate for it. Simply put, it is the truth of who God is and who we are in relationship with him. As we focus in on God's goodness, much of our work is like that of my great-grandfather, mining through all the hard rock to find what he was looking for. When it comes to messages about who we are, the mining process feels the same. There is much out there claiming to be true, but God's voice has been clear throughout time about who we are as people. We are created, we've separated, and we can be reconciled and redeemed. It is this process on repeat that is the gospel, the Good News, lived out in our daily experiences.

Darkness Helps Us See the Light

We recognize that if there is a force for goodness in the world (God), there must be a counterforce, because we are hardly living in symbiotic, peaceful times. This thread of despair has been consistent throughout history. Scripture tells the story of the force/counterforce and the separation in the garden. Fallout has consistently happened since. We all experience the opposite of goodness. This is the separation part of the big story.

I may have never seen a devil with a pitchfork, but I've seen the destruction caused by abuse, addiction, disease, and division. The counterforce is real. It also does not have to win. The light can always overcome the darkness. Does that mean we don't die from disease? That reconciliation always takes place? No. It means God's goodness does not bend to our current experience of the counterforce. Even when life is crumbling around us, God's unchanging nature is just that—steady and unwavering—and good. It is what we can cling to with confidence when nothing else seems right or safe. If anything is true about this life, it's that we will experience hardship. After all, Jesus said, "I have told you these things, so that in me you may have peace. In this world you will have trouble. But take heart! I have overcome the world" (John 16:33).

You're probably thinking, *What in the world? I thought this was a book about seeking out goodness!* It is. Which is why we must acknowledge that the opposite of good exists. Thankfully Jesus is good news in what can feel like a world of nothing but bad news. Just like with my neighbor's tree and the contrast between branches and sky, the contrast between hope and despair helps us focus in on one or the other. In fact, almost every good thing can be twisted into something harmful. The counterforce's best tool is twisting what was meant for good into something used for harm. When we are able to separate the good from the evil intent, we may even find that what Satan used for harm can bring clarity around what God created for good.

Once we remember that God's nature is loving, that he is with us today as much as yesterday and will remain with us into tomorrow, we are better positioned to see the

Write down some things that have pained you recently:

Griefs

Disappointments

Unmet expectations

Consider where Jesus was during those moments. Where is he now in relation to you?

How has he provided for you in the midst of your pain?

How have others helped care for you?

What good has contrasted with the heartache? Make a list of the light in the midst of the dark.

world with a lens of truth. Our vantage point is closer to his and is one of grace. It doesn't mean we don't see all the destruction, chaos, and even evil around us. Quite the opposite—the contrast provides clarity we all can use. Our vision comes into focus as we contrast the light with the dark and see the good.

What We Consume

This is the information age, where we can Google anything and get some type of answer. Even the fact that we use *Google* as a verb, meaning "to look for an answer on the internet and trust the internet to help me find that answer," is telling. Case in point: last night at dinner we were talking to our girls about memorizing the Lord's Prayer, and they asked why we should when we can just Google it. (Insert the face-palm emoji here.) But this reminds us that we now have immediate answers available at our fingertips. Whether they are true or not is what we need to discern.

Doctors often ask patients with a new diagnosis to avoid the temptation to go home and Google the disease. Why? They don't want their patients seeing the most dramatic pictures, hearing the worst stories, and consuming the grimmest statistics without context. A doctor who knows a patient's overall health or underlying conditions can paint a more specific and realistic picture of how a given diagnosis will impact that individual. The information available on the internet may technically be true, but it's irrelevant to a given patient's reality. A physician cannot guarantee that the statistics a scared person finds at 2:00 a.m. on a random website will be helpful. Do we fault the patient for wanting to know? Of course not.

There is a reason the phrase "knowledge is power" has withstood time. When we have truth, we can walk into situations with more power to make sound decisions based on reality. Our confidence goes up and our responses are better informed when we bring truth with us into any moment. The question is, *Is our knowledge based in truth?*

If we rush to consume whatever we can find about a given topic without much regard for the source or the quality, we may end up like the patient at 2:00 a.m. who decides they only have two months to live because they read a random account on an even more random blog. Unfortunately, our own confirmation bias, the willingness to believe information that confirms an opinion or belief system you already hold, creates self-perpetuating echo chambers where we are drawn to stories that confirm what we already believe. Social media is a beast in this way. We get caught in a tornado of information that spins us in circles around a single core belief. The only way out is to stop and evaluate our source of truth.

Jesus quoted Deuteronomy when he said, "It is written: 'Man shall not live on bread alone, but on every word that comes from the mouth of God'" (Matt. 4:4). The more we know the truth of God's Word, the more accurately we will be able to interpret the real-life situations in our lives. Coworker tensions. Parenting strategies. School fundraiser debates. Church budget decisions. Scripture can inform every dilemma, but we usually need to take in other information as well. There is no book in the Bible that clearly spells out how we should vote, who we should marry, or what we should make for dinner that is both gluten-free and delicious. We have to use our knowledge base from other sources too.

A famous quote attributed to theologian Karl Barth is "We must hold the Bible in one hand and the newspaper in the other." The original quote is found in *Time* magazine and reads, "Take your Bible and take your newspaper, and read both. But interpret newspapers from your Bible."[1] Scripture holds the eternal perspective. So though we use all available sources in our pursuit of truth, we know that the metanarrative of the gospel is reflected in what is true. Creation, separation, reconciliation, and redemption are woven through our lives. In any given situation, we can ask, Does this reflect

God's creation? Humanity's fall? Jesus drawing people to himself and making all things new? If it does not, what part of the story are we missing? We can then search that piece out so we can have a bigger picture of what is true.

Taking In New Information, or the Burned Bacon Principle

"You let me do this before! Why won't you now?" Every parent has heard some form of this argument. Our children crave consistency, so when we change our rules or permissions, they want (with good reason) to know why. "I have new information" is a common response in my house. I heard the sassy tone of the characters on that TV show; I learned there won't be any parents at that party; I found out you consider barbecue potato chips "lunch." As I gather new information as a parent, I have the freedom and good sense to change my mind.

We are constantly taking in new information that helps us see the truth. Whether it's the information we consume or the input from all five of our senses, we are in a continuous state of evaluating the world for what is true. Burning bacon can act as a guide. The smells in my kitchen can tell me when bacon turns from cooking to burning. When this happens I take the pan out of the oven because I am acting on this new information. However, if I ignore the new truth (the smell) and hold on to my old belief that the bacon is doing just fine, I won't be facing the reality in front of me that the bacon is indeed burning. I am presented with new information but still living in my old belief system. We call this denial.

41

God gives us this incredible body and brain to interact with the world. We are to use our brains to make informed, discerning decisions. To hold on to the old bacon narrative because it better fits our preconceived ideas of what breakfast will and should look like doesn't help us understand reality or think on what is true. So why might I want to keep the old narrative alive?

I like the old version better. *(Unburned bacon is what I pictured this morning.)*

I don't want to admit I was wrong. *(I made a mistake and let the bacon burn.)*

I am afraid of what others will think. *(Bad moms burn bacon.)*

Obviously I'm taking the bacon analogy further than it needs to go, but replace bacon with any area of your life where you are taking in new information that points to a different conclusion, and you may be having the same feelings. Humility is our key to growth. It reminds us that we don't know everything. Therefore, it is natural and normal for us to be wrong sometimes, and we don't need to be embarrassed when we are. What is actually embarrassing is serving a plate of burned, blackened bacon and pretending it is delicious or even edible. Things don't go well when we let pride get in the way of recognizing what is true.

So as we take in new information and find that what we thought was true may not be, we can use our God-given minds and change them. If we pursue truth—what is real and not imagined—and think on it, we are promised a more peaceful existence. Back to Philippians 4:9: "Put into practice what you learned from me, what you heard and saw and realized. Do that, and God, who makes everything work together, will work you into his most excellent harmonies" (MSG). God is not in the business of asking us to pretend burned bacon is good. When we face and accept what is true and work within truth's boundaries, we are more likely to experience his goodness.

When I read stories of the disciples, I often think of them working with the information they had in the moment. The conversations they had with Jesus and one another seem silly to many of us who read Scripture today and have a different vantage point for the stories. We have a broader view

QUESTIONS TO CONSIDER WHEN PRESENTED WITH NEW INFORMATION

>> Does this new information reinforce what I already knew and believed?
>> Does it conflict with what I believed before?
>> Does it come from a trusted source?
>> Does it line up with the metanarrative of creation, separation, reconciliation, and redemption?
>> What new insights can I gain with this information? About God? Myself? The world?
>> How is this new information revealing goodness?

of who Jesus is because we know the cross is coming. We also know about the resurrection. When we read about the disciples with their real-time questions, we can understand that they were making decisions with limited information. Though they were walking with, sleeping next to, and eating with Jesus, they knew him only through their vantage point in history. As the story unfolds, we see them being presented with new information and their understanding broadening. They have a choice to either cling to the old understanding of Jesus or incorporate new information to better know him and his plan for them and the world.

The disciples remind us that we are not alone in our limited understanding of what is true. It is the human condition in many ways. God is God and we are not. Though we are called to think on what is true, at the same time we recognize that our view of the world is limited by our human capacity.

Recognizing Fake News

I was up late one night and noticed that a number of my friends had posted the same video on Facebook. The video's title was compelling and disputed the headlines of the day. It was framed as information people weren't hearing on mainstream media and therefore something everyone must pay attention to. One of the friends who shared was Molly. I watched the video because she shared it. I find her to be a thoughtful, faithful woman who loves her neighbors. But as I watched, I had some questions. Some details just didn't add up.

The next morning I saw that Molly posted a second message on Facebook, stating that she regretted posting the video and was asking for forgiveness. This is part of what she said:

> Truth matters and we are all hungry for it, but desperation
> for truth can make us vulnerable to ingesting poison dressed
> like a delicacy. Like I said in my post yesterday, the need
> for wisdom and discernment in the days ahead cannot be
> overstated, and we are all susceptible to it. If we think we
> are beyond being deceived or are unwilling to receive cor-
> rection, we are more vulnerable to it.

Molly experienced the compelling draw of confirmation bias. Online logarithms are designed to give us headlines we will click on based on our online history. The internet knows what we like and gladly hands it to us regardless of whether it's true or not. Confirmation bias is a strong draw for all of us. It strokes our egos and tells us, "You were right all along." That sounds an awful lot like a snake in a garden that told those first two people, "You know best. Follow your instincts." (My paraphrase.)

Our "information sources" feel less reliable these days. Though journalists have always reported with their personal biases influencing their storytelling, the current sensational-izing of every headline leaves us searching for sources that give facts and allow us to draw our own conclusions. We have to take responsibility to pay closer attention to sources and know who is feeding us information. It can be exhausting, but when we stop paying attention, we are more susceptible to believing fake news. This vigilance will ultimately help us see what is good.

Fake news doesn't just permeate our media waves; it can run through our heads as well. Just like in the garden at the beginning of humanity's story, we hear whispers of doubt about who God is and who we are in relationship to him. It can be as simple as "You can do this on your own," causing us to have an inflated sense of self, or "You're not cut out for this," leaving us feeling helpless and hopeless. Neither of these extremes is true. These false narratives are why it is essential that we remember what God says is true of us. Mining through our news feed in all its forms and cutting the fake news will help us see what is true with more clarity.

Two Things Can Be True at Once

The fake news of the day includes false dichotomies. We are often presented with opposite viewpoints and told one must be true and the other not. Snake alert. This is the enemy offering us wrong thinking through a limited paradigm. We are complex people with complex opinions and realities. We can find that two (or more) things can be true at once. God didn't make us one-dimensional. What is true of us as people is that we can hold many truths in tension. Jesus held multiple truths at the same time and always went back to the larger truth that God creates, restores, and redeems.

I had a carful of girls, and we headed to one of my favorite spots in our city, the Denver Art Museum. Not only is the museum a great place to wander; it's also a reason for us to take the ten-minute drive into downtown. For my city kids to step outside the familiarity of our neighborhood to see and experience a broader circle of people, buildings, and life than our ordinary is the kind of adventure I'm almost always up for.

Make a list of the ways you consume information. Rank the amount of time and attention you give each source from most to least. Now rank the credibility of each source from most to least. How do these two align? Where do adjustments need to be made so that the information you are consuming reflects truth?

I started circling the museum's block, looking for an on-street parking spot. I turned the corner, and the block ahead was lined with tents between the curb and the sidewalk. The headlines of the last few weeks depicted the city administration's dilemma of where to allow the homeless residents to sleep. The public right-of-way between street and sidewalk had become a common spot, and apparently the block I was driving down was one of the newest pop-up camping villages. Despite ample curbside parking along the row of tents, I continued driving down the street and parked in front of a restaurant with patrons sitting outside eating. The disparities in our city suddenly felt stark and obvious. I was feeling the tension of being pulled between multiple truths at once. Here were a few:

- I was excited to visit this world-class, well-funded museum with these girls.
- My fellow city dwellers were enjoying an outdoor summer lunch on the sidewalk. Saturday afternoon cocktails and conversations around job changes were flowing.
- My fellow city dwellers were also sitting in tents across the street. It was the middle of the day, and they had nowhere else to go.
- As we walked by the restaurant, we took pictures in front of its outdoor mural. The colors were vibrant and the words strong: "Love This City."

Which was true? Do we love this city? Or do we lack the collective will to figure out how to better serve our homeless neighbors? The tension was hinting that both couldn't be true at the same time. And yet both were.

Two things can be true at once. I've been saying that a lot the last few years. As we are presented with either/or options where we must choose between extremes, it's good to remember that life is layered and complicated.

- I can like chocolate AND vanilla ice cream.
- I can love who my kids are becoming AND be sad they're growing up.
- I can vote a certain party or candidate AND not agree with their entire platform.
- I can be annoyed at my husband's night-owl tendencies AND appreciate a quiet house in the morning.
- I can believe God is good AND have a hard time trusting his will for me is better than my own.

In fact, the gospel is full of both/and.

- Jesus was fully human AND fully divine.
- I am predisposed to go against God's will (sin), AND he loves me (grace).
- I want to be recognized and validated for being capable, AND Jesus says the last shall be first.
- I work to avoid disappointment and pain, AND God will use all things to work together for good.

We can pretend the world is framed in such a way that we must choose, but if we are searching for the truth, we must recognize that it is more often bent toward a framework of both/and than either/or. I can find goodness in people and not agree with every decision they have made or will make. I can trust God in this process of finding goodness and worry that I will be disappointed. I can attempt to offer the world my most excellent work and strive for humility at the same time. Outside of the either/or paradigm, we have freedom to find truth in more places.

Back to our downtown adventure to the museum. How do I think on multiple things that are true at once? I pause and recognize the reality that is there. I was looking forward to being at the museum. It is a place with lots of resources. I did think sitting at a café table having a beer on a summer afternoon sounded nice. I desperately wanted my homeless neighbors to have choices and safety and housing. I did love my city. All things were true in that moment. I didn't have to deny one feeling, thought, or fact to validate another. I did need to acknowledge each one and not rush through the feelings that the tension produced. I could then surrender the truth to God. Call it a prayer, if you will, though in my case that sounds more structured and articulated than it actually was. It was more of a recognition in spirit that the world is full of contrasting forces and realities, and I am the kitchen anthropologist standing in the middle of them.

God Has Not Left Us: God Is Good All the Time

There is an old call and response I learned years ago at our church in Portland. Common in the African American church, the call helps a group of believers collectively remember and reflect back to one another that God's goodness does not change.

Pastor: God is good . . .

Congregation: All the time.

Pastor: All the time . . .

Congregation: God is good.

There is something about reminding one another of the truth that reawakens our senses. I picture generations of Black churchgoers reminding one another of this truth when everything around them felt like it was on fire. The truth that God is good is what we can cling to when life feels like nothing but bad news. We can take heart that in a world of difficult circumstances, the truth remains that God created us, loves us, has drawn us to himself, and redeemed us in Christ. This is good and this is true.

Finally, we reflect this goodness back to the world with our actions and our words. The Christian faith is built on the testimony of eyewitnesses, after all—men and women who saw Jesus crucified, saw him die, and then most certainly saw him alive again. These people then went and told others what they had seen and experienced. This is how the Good News has spread for generations around the world. We learn about God's goodness, we experience it, and then we share it. Seeking, finding, and reflecting God's truth and goodness in a world that feels dark and difficult is part of the Christian call.

A Prayer for
WHATEVER IS TRUE

In the search for what is true, we come to you, Father.
We come with our questions, doubts, and unsure
  responses.
We come as people wandering the desert (and suburbs
  and city streets and nature trails).
We come with earnest hearts and preconceived ideas.
We come with as much humility as we can muster this
  side of heaven.

Lord, open our minds to the things you would have us
  know.
Give us ears to hear new insights with a fresh spirit,
Eyes to see your world, your people, your truth with an
  intense clarity.
Holy Spirit, help us to distinguish between the voice of
  our heavenly Father and all the noise that surrounds
  us.

Jesus, we know you are the way, the truth, and the life.
All things begin and end in you.
And yet there are decisions to be made, votes to be cast,
  and relationships to walk through.
It is hard to know what is true in the murk of the daily
  muck.

We lean in deep to what we know to be certain of you
    when so many details feel unclear.
Thank you for always welcoming us with your gentle,
    loving arms.
This we know is true.

Holy Spirit, we ask for your guidance in every space and
    conversation.
Be our filter as we seek what is true in this world so that
    we may experience your refreshing goodness in new
    ways.
Quicken our spirits when we encounter truth.
Help us to recognize what is from God so that we may
    also know what is not.
Lead us toward the places and people who will give us
    wisdom that is more than facts but is the truth of the
    world.
Comfort us when we don't find the answers we are
    looking for or are disappointed and grieved by what
    is true.
Lead us in the darkness to places of light so that we
    might catch a glimpse of hope before night comes
    again.

With humble hearts we pray.

Amen.

QUESTIONS *for* REFLECTION

1. When have you been surprised by truth?

2. What does *fake news* mean to you? Where do you tend to hear it? Is your fake news different from someone else's?

3. How do you actively seek out new information? Where might you be pretending the bacon isn't burned?

4. Where have you experienced two things to be true at the same time? How did it feel to acknowledge that reality?

5. Where do you see the pattern of creation, separation, reconciliation, and redemption playing out in your life right now?

When Hope Is Hidden

I opened my Bible, believing there had to be some discouraged soul in its pages who shared my unease. I know the book is full of stories of flawed, hungry characters who have doubts, cravings, regrets, and all kinds of shortcomings. The people are comforting because they're real and make big mistakes (not just the little, polite ones), and then they have to figure out how to live in the midst of their mess-ups. There had to be someone in all those pages who went looking for hope in desperation and came out on the winning end.

Who went looking for Jesus? The Bible stories flipped through my mind like cards in a card catalog: the bleeding woman, Zacchaeus, Jairus. They all went looking for Jesus and found him right where they thought he'd be: surrounded by the crowd, the paparazzi of the day. It was like a tourist in Hawaii looking for the good beach. It was obvious, there, right in the open, easy to find.

That easy find isn't as relatable these days. I want to find hope where it's hard to see, in the fog and even in the darkness. I want to find Jesus where he's hidden. I'm certain I'm not the first.

In deciding on the title for this book, I did some wordsmithing. "Searching" sounds a little more like my everyday word choice. Really, I look for things. I don't "seek out" my car keys unless I'm feeling especially British or colonial. But what I found was that when you *search* for something, you aren't sure it even exists; you're not confident you'll find it. For example, you search the horizon for land (I guess I am feeling a little colonial today after all), you scan the distant view, unsure if the land is there. But when you *seek out* something, you know it exists; you just need to figure out how to find it.

So back to flipping through my mental card catalog. Of course! Why didn't I think of her sooner? My all-time favorite, Mary Magdalene, was the first to see Jesus raised from the dead. She went looking for his body and found him alive and well. But it wasn't instant recognition, and it wasn't without some dark moments of the soul when she didn't know which side was up. Quite the opposite—she was almost annoyed, mad even, at him when he tried to reveal himself to her.

When Jesus appeared to Mary Magdalene outside his tomb, she didn't recognize him right away. In fact, it was her grief that kept her from seeing the very one she was looking for. When she found the empty tomb, she assumed the worst—that someone had stolen her beloved teacher's body—when in reality the very person she was looking for was standing right next to her. Her tears blurred and compromised her vision, but Jesus's familiar voice caught her attention. She couldn't initially see it was him, but then, because she had spent so much time with him leading up to that point, she recognized him. Jesus then gave her instructions to go and tell the good thing she had seen.

Mary's faith brought her to look for Jesus. Though she was looking in the right place, she was looking for the wrong form. She was thinking she would find a corpse; she wasn't expecting a breathing, standing, moving man. The hard circumstances of her life kept her from initially recognizing him when he was right in front of her. But her extended time with him before his death gave her a familiarity that allowed her to recognize his voice even when she wasn't expecting it. First, she had to be willing to take in new information and acknowledge that she'd been wrong. Once she found what was true, she was surprised, delighted by the reality that Jesus was in fact much nearer than she'd thought.

Finally, she ran to tell the others the good and unexpected way she'd encountered God. A way that in fact changed her understanding about who he was. She now had a bigger understanding of what was true.

Mary's story can act as a blueprint for our seeking and finding goodness in the world. Goodness is often presented in ways we're not expecting. It takes us by surprise. And it often happens in the midst of our darkest grief. The true and beautiful can be right in front of us, but we cannot recognize it until we listen for and hear God's voice.

Part 2

CANCELING
CANCEL CULTURE

Whatever is noble . . .

PHILIPPIANS 4:8

*Everyone needs to be valued. Everyone has
the potential to give something back.*

PRINCESS DIANA

It took a few hours before the messages started arriving in my DMs. I'd posted a photo in my Instagram stories about the notable news of the day. It was a political moment, but I didn't feel as though the post itself was political. I was just emotional about the historic significance. That was it. No endorsement. A simple recognition that history was being made and my daughters were watching (literally, on

59

the TV). I received a number of celebratory responses, but the messages started getting nasty to the point where readers and friends essentially said, "That's it! I thought I could trust you. But no more. I'm done." I posted something that I believed was pretty benign, pretty neutral (no one could deny this was a historic moment), and I was being canceled.

We've all felt it—the big cancel. We can almost hear the *Family Feud* buzzer go off with the red *X*s floating above our heads. At least on *Family Feud* you get three strikes before you're out. No longer. One sentiment that halfway says we're excited about an event, person, trend, or belief and we're done. We have been dismissed because something we've said has not fit into someone else's worldview or paradigm. The opposite may also be true—that we've written someone off as irrelevant because of the way they voted, what they believe on a particular topic, or even the words they used when describing a moment. We've quietly acquiesced to a culture of nitpicking and moral policing each other to death.

As we consider "whatever is noble," knights and fairy tales come to my mind. I would say someone who is "noble" is of incredible character or courage. The New Living Translation replaces *noble* with *honorable*. That feels a bit more palpable to my modern, everyday experiences. I can still search out those things that are honorable and find them.

Sometimes finding the honorable is easy. We know what is good and right in another person or situation, and we can call it out. Sometimes the honorable is difficult to find, but searching for it certainly helps us find goodness. We can honor people, traditions, ways of thinking, and God's creation. By honoring, we are recognizing the effort or contribution someone or something has made to the greater good.

Why consider what is noble or honorable in someone else? How does that show us more of God's goodness? Because it helps us see how God is uniquely reflected in every person. Those good qualities that your offensive neighbor or uncle has are the tint of God, as if God colored your uncle with generosity or joy even though he may tell jokes you find inappropriate. Our job in looking for the honorable means that we aren't silencing someone because of one part of who they are. We are recognizing that the parts we don't like are only a portion of the person.

The quiet Instagram unfollows I received that day were a form of canceling. People no longer wanted to hear what I had to say. That had a certain level of implicit rejection because it didn't honor my complexity. The direct messages and texts were more pointed, more personal. Some people approached me with a genuine curiosity I appreciated—a "tell me more" attitude with an "I appreciate your thoughts" closing. But the messages that hurt were from friends who doubted my integrity and my faith. I sat in that pain for a bit and then asked myself, *Where would Jesus be in this conversation? What would his words of life be for this person? How can I honor the years of relationship I've had with this friend, even though she isn't offering me the same?* It took discipline because I was hurt and still didn't believe I had done anything wrong. But it was the right way to move forward.

In a time when we are drawing lines in the sand over the hot issues of the day, we are ready to get angry, offended, or outraged over the latest take. We are equally ready to dismiss or "cancel" the person who stands on the other side of our self-created lines. We are offered false binaries, and we step into them when we know the issues may be more nuanced. There is a better response, one that values people's intents and searches for truth without canceling them if they come to different conclusions. Disagreement can be healthy. God gives us free will, after all, to think and come to our own decisions. In the gospel, unity moves us toward one another even when we have nuanced and varied ideas about more peripheral topics. Unity involves mutual respect. When we silence a dissenting voice over a single opinion, stance, lifestyle choice, or theological viewpoint, we are denying their dignity and even humanity. As followers of Christ, we can continue to recognize the *imago Dei* in one another while disagreeing on some things. Acceptance does not have to mean total agreement or denial of our own beliefs but rather offering a third way of honor and trust.

We Really Like to Be Right

Cancel culture is how history books will remember the tone of our era. We were people who had little tolerance for ideas outside of our own, they will say, and because of that we missed the rich life that comes from diverse thought. We automatically put people into categories that we then deem "good" or "bad." From theology to simple catchphrases to where people shop or don't, everything and everyone has become an issue that we can stand behind or against.

Apart from Christ, there is no perfect solution, voting record, or moral character. We forget that kind people can have bad ideas, and conversely good ideas can come from people we'd rather not hang out with. We like to categorize people into "right" or "wrong" because it helps us make sense of a chaotic world and feel a little better about ourselves. The truth is we all fall short. When speaking to an audience of young adults, former President Obama said, "If I tweet or hashtag about how you didn't do something right or used the wrong verb, then I can sit back and feel pretty good about myself. . . . If all you're doing is casting stones, you're probably not going to get that far."[1]

Of course, the language of casting stones takes us to the famous story in John 8 of Jesus in the temple courts. A woman caught in adultery is dragged by the religious leaders into the scene. They explain to Jesus that technically they're allowed to stone her. The law says so. Essentially, "We get to cancel her!" Here is how Jesus responds:

> Jesus bent down and wrote with his finger in the dirt. They kept at him, badgering him. He straightened up and said, "The sinless one among you, go first: Throw the stone." Bending down again, he wrote some more in the dirt.
>
> Hearing that, they walked away, one after another, beginning with the oldest. The woman was left alone. Jesus stood up and spoke to her. "Woman, where are they? Does no one condemn you?"
>
> "No one, Master."
>
> "Neither do I," said Jesus. "Go on your way. From now on, don't sin." (John 8:6–11 MSG)

Jesus leads with honor because he sees the woman as more than her sin in that moment. She would have been an easy woman to cancel. In fact, the mob was already saying her action disqualified her from being treated well. Jesus could have simply said, "No, that's not right," but instead he turned it back to the accusers, as if to say, "Really? You are all blameless then? You've never done anything wrong? Ever?"

There is something in us that wants to be right and catch others doing wrong. We've collectively created a culture where we're affirmed by putting others down. This is not operating out of God's goodness. Our first job in fighting today's cancel culture is to examine our own motives to cancel someone else. We may not act on canceling those who disagree with us, but I'd guess most of us are tempted to prove others wrong in order to prove ourselves right from time to time. In these moments we must pause and ask ourselves some honest questions about our motives and our fears.

QUESTIONS TO CONSIDER WHEN FEELING THE NEED TO PROVE SOMEONE WRONG

» What am I afraid of?
» What qualities of or contributions from this person can I honor?
» What can I further think on? Does this mean I should wait to respond?
» Does my disagreement with this person disqualify him or her from every part of my life?
» Am I in a position to cast a stone here?

Major on the Majors

My sister-in-law Lindsay works at a church about forty minutes from our house. A few years ago a couple from her congregation was moving to our neighborhood, and Lindsay asked me and my husband, Derek, if we had any church recommendations for them. That's all it took for us to start firing out the questions. "Are they complementarian or egalitarian?" "How do they feel about women in the pulpit?" "Do they want LGBTQ+ affirming or an orthodox view on marriage?" "Do they want multigenerational? Multiethnic? Multilanguage? Or hipster vibe?" "Are they wanting 'Spirit-led' or three-point sermons?" We had our local churches categorized and cataloged in our heads by positions on various issues and demographics of attendees. Just the way Jesus would like it, I'm sure. We assumed this couple would have their yes and no columns for how each of these questions would impact whether the church was the "right fit."

Twenty-three years ago Derek and I sat through a new members class at our church in Portland, Oregon. Not having grown up in church, I'd never been an official member of a congregation. I was naive about church politics. When describing the church during this class, the pastor said that we "major on the majors," meaning there are a few key tenets to Christianity that we agree on, and how we then move forward to understand other questions of faith can leave us in different places. I liked that. But it also felt confusing. If we were congregating around a common belief system, how much division could there be? (I did say "naive," didn't I?)

I've since learned one person's minor is another's major. Even deciding on what the majors are can feel exhausting.

Every part of the American church is participating in this type of splintering, whether through denominational breaks or within specific congregations or even family units. Our understanding of what Jesus meant when he said certain things or what the larger arc of Scripture indicates can leave us in disagreement.

Disagreements about trivial things, like favorite TV shows or the best salsa recipes, can easily be put in the category of personal preference. But when the disagreements are about who God is, how he operates, or how he calls us to live out our days on earth, the differences can feel monumental and personal. These are not simply about comedy versus action or how much onion should be added. These are questions of salvation and eternity.

I understand why we fight for our beliefs with such passion. However, we get tempted in these places to respond with a righteous canceling. No matter where we stand on any splintering issue, if we feel we understand God's directives correctly and differently from our neighbor but aren't working to understand our neighbor's perspective, we are trending more toward the religious scholars and Pharisees that led the adulterous woman to Jesus than we are toward Jesus. We can't miss that the people ready to cancel her were the religious leaders coming from a point of self-proclaimed moral superiority. Yet when Jesus called them out, they recognized their own sin and hypocrisy. They knew they were ready to pummel this woman with rocks. It would have felt satisfying, righteous even. Her wrongness would have made them feel justified and superior.

Jesus didn't just draw that line in the sand for those religious leaders in that moment. He did it for all of us throughout time. The temptation to cancel is part of our sinful nature. It is not searching out God's goodness or honoring the image bearers around us. It is born from a place of wanting to feel superior. Argh. Yuck. And true at the same time. The challenge in front of us is to recognize our own pride and need to be right and walk away from casting stones.

We Remember What We're Looking For

Just as we seek out goodness, we can seek out the worst in people too. I don't like to admit it, but we can have confirmation bias toward people we disagree with. We read articles or post video clips just so we can show how wrong someone is. We roll our eyes behind someone's back (or sometimes to their face) when they start talking on a given subject because we know where the conversation is headed. We, of course, already believe they are wrong.

We have control over this, though it may not feel like we do (retweeting those zinger tweets is so tempting!). We can stop and remember that a starting place for seeking out goodness is looking for common ground. It is a renewing of the mind to consciously change direction. Looking for the worst in people is not our aim. That doesn't mean things don't need to be challenged or behaviors don't need to be held accountable, but listening to someone just so you can point out all the ways they are wrong is neither redeeming nor helpful. We are seeking out goodness, after all.

The opposite of honor is dismissal—to push something aside, to not give it any consideration because we have perceived it has little to no value. We can dismiss a person, an institution, a place, a food group, anything based on one small trait. Some things are worth more, so when we dismiss them, there are larger consequences. If I dismiss a home when on a house search because it is on a busy street, there is not the same moral punch as dismissing another person because of a lifestyle choice. People are made in God's image and matter the most. Embodied souls should not be treated as material things, yet we live in a culture that objectifies and dehumanizes in the way we communicate. To be countercultural as a follower of Jesus is to honor people with passion and intensity so there is no room to question that they matter.

Why did it sting so deeply when friends sent me canceling texts? By dismissing someone because of a single view or behavior, we are diminishing their value. It may not be intentional, but our words sting when we are not honoring the other person's *imago Dei*, God's image portrayed in them. Our baseline must always be the human dignity inherently given by God. A person's worth is not determined by how they line up with our approved metrics but rather by the fact that they are made in God's image. If we begin there and keep coming back to that starting place, we will do the important work of dismantling cancel culture. This is the very work of seeking out goodness.

Canceling versus Accountability

It is healthy for us to hold one another to account, to say there is a collective expectation of how we are to behave. Jesus told the woman in the temple courts, "From now on, don't sin." There is a place for saying something is wrong or inappropriate. However, cancel culture takes one thing someone says that the group does not agree with and uses it as ammunition. It's an excuse to dismiss anything good or helpful a person may have to offer in any other area of life and work. Accountability, on the other hand, leads with the presumption that the person (or organization) is valuable, that a misstep or a misspoken word is part of the human experience. When perfection is the standard, it's impossible for any of us to live up to it. Eventually the end result will be canceling everyone. If we are to move forward in health, we need both the space to make mistakes and receive counsel and correction and the opportunity to still be honored as God's beloved. This is God's big story living itself out in community.

So how do we create a community or relationship where accountability can thrive? How do we offer one another healthy ways of improving when mistakes are made? How do we call for change in a way that shows a behavior or practice is unacceptable without canceling the entire person? Especially in a culture where others make big missteps without consequences?

Here are a few guiding principles when we feel correction is called for but canceling is not:

Affirm what is good. In parenting, supervising, and any relationship where feedback is offered, the sandwich method is often implemented—a compliment followed by correction, followed by another celebration of what the person is doing right. It's a technique that recognizes we all need a little affirmation to be able to hear the correction. When we offer feedback this way, we are recognizing the person or

organization is not *all* bad but rather has areas for
improvement within the context of general good
work.

State existing and aspirational goals. It helps to remind
everyone involved what the goal is when giving correction. "You want to love your spouse well." "You
want to treat all employees fairly." "You want to
speak in a way people will listen." When we state
out loud what the larger hope is, we are reminding
everyone what the specific suggestion is intended to
move toward.

Consider the relationship. The closer we are to a person,
the more authority our voice should have in their
life. A person's spouse has a different level of knowledge, intimacy, and responsibility than a pastor or a
boss. However, a boss is expected to keep employees
accountable to the responsibilities and qualities of
their work. The relationship determines the type of
accountability that is appropriate. We need to ask
ourselves, *Am I the right person to speak about this topic
to this particular person?*

Consider public versus private conversations. This is also
determined by the nature of the relationship. Personal accountability is for trusted advisers. In an
era when more and more people have public platforms, more public conversations are taking place
on social media. When a person puts themselves in
a public position, a public conversation is appropriate. However, our role in that conversation should
be guided by the question, *Am I loving God and*

*others more by calling out this person/group in the way
that I am?*

Lead with the fruit of the Spirit. Kindness, gentleness, and
self-control are traits we can bring to any conversation. However, we can only display them in limited
quantities in our own strength and merit. That is
where the Holy Spirit must do the incredible work of
giving us portions beyond our own doing. In order for
us to live this fruit, our spiritual roots must be deep.

Maintain consequences. Though we are honoring each
other, we still have to own up to what we've done
and face the impact. If someone has broken trust,
they must repair it. A relationship may never go
back to the way it was. A marriage may not survive
infidelity. We can honor each other and set up
healthy boundaries. Conflict, when done well, can
lead to intimacy. So though discipline may be required, in the end there can still be a stronger trust.

Remember that mutual is best. The integrity of the process
requires all parties to be invested in doing what is
good and healthy. In a marriage, both commit to
be faithful. In a team, everyone commits to work
hard. In a church body, we commit to praying for
one another. We can certainly honor someone when
they are disrespectful toward us—that is the way of
Christ. However, we can't demand honor when we
are unwilling to extend it.

In part 1, I told you about my friend Molly. She posted
a video on Facebook and, after being approached by some

friends, posted an apology the next day. This is part of what she wrote in her follow-up apology post:

> We need each other. I hold deep gratitude for my friends who reached out to me yesterday to share their perspectives, expertise and information they discovered upon further research which helped uncover areas I was blind to and desperately needed them to help me see. They were kind, professional, humble and helpful in their approach, and I'm grateful for friends who help correct my missteps with gentleness rather than the air of superiority, hatred and anger that we so often see in these spaces.

Molly was able to hear the corrections from her friends because they were honoring in their delivery. "Kind, professional, humble and helpful." When her friends were determining how to honor Molly in their correction, I'm sure they were thinking about who she is. She is kind, thoughtful, and gentle. They extended her the same respect they knew she would offer them if the tables were turned. This is the mutual part. Many of these reach-outs were in private. They weren't excited to "gotcha" comment on her original post to show their superior knowledge but instead privately asked her, "Have you considered this?" I want more friends like these, who see my blind spots and gently nudge me toward a better way of thinking, presenting, and living. This is what it is to honor one another.

Different Starting Places

I walked into the group unsure of what to expect. I casually knew these women from soccer carpools and band concerts, and we were in this meeting because of a shared common interest. We lived in the same neighborhood, sent our children to the same schools, in many ways made the same choices for our lives. And yet I knew my worldview

QUESTIONS TO CONSIDER WHEN HOLDING SOMEONE ACCOUNTABLE

» What is it about this issue that makes me think it needs to be addressed? Is it going against a Scripture directive?

» How are my feelings impacting my views on the topic? Am I able to look at this objectively? Do I need to wait twenty-four hours to respond?

» How genuinely curious am I about the other person's position?

» Is this an issue that will harm the credibility of the gospel if it is not addressed?

» Is this an issue that will harm people or my relationship with the other person if it is not addressed?

» Am I the one to speak to this person on this topic? If so, what is the most honoring method?

» Where would Jesus be standing in this conversation? What would he want this person to know? How can I offer that message in my own voice with my own words?

was unique to many of theirs. My motivation to be part of the conversation was different. I wasn't sure how I would be received.

The question of whether to go and be part of the conversation came down to this: Does the starting place matter? Does it matter if we are coming at a subject, a project, or a plan from different motivations? Or does it matter that we care about the same issue?

There is something comforting in being with people who are approaching a problem with the same underlying drive. A few years ago I went on a trip for Christian women writers to visit the Texas-Mexico border and learn about US government family separation policies happening there. Meeting these sisters of the heart who were equally motivated by their faith, their belief in the *imago Dei*, and their interest in immigration issues had an element of freedom. I could bring my whole self. I didn't need to hold back, worry that I was using too many Christian references in my language, or worry that I was caring about my neighbors in a way other Christians may find too political. In other words, these were my people.

Just because I'm more comfortable in certain crowds doesn't mean I should avoid others. Jesus was the great example on this front. Not only was his core group of disciples—those he hung out with most—a diverse bunch, but he was the one who brought them together. How incredible would it be if we the church were the ones who brought people together? Some of us are great at it, but most of us could use a little practice at spending time with people who approach life from different vantage points and inviting them into our spaces to experience one another.

Back to the group of neighborhood women. I told myself I was going to listen. I wasn't going to talk too much. I truly was there to learn, yet I had a lot of thoughts on the topic at hand. I did listen, and I learned. I also talked more than I'd planned. I brought all of myself, which meant I didn't hide my faith as my motivation to be there. I honored my own tradition in that way. And I could read the room. It made some people uncomfortable. Would I say the things I said again? Yes. Would I say them in the way I said them? I think so. Am I glad I went even though my motivations were different? Absolutely. Did I honor the other women in the process? I hope so.

To not have gone because of preconceived ideas or opinions on my end would not have been honoring. Being part of the group, asking questions, listening, and trying to hear not only what was said but also what was unsaid were also honoring. When we consider what it means to honor someone else, we can think speeches, parades, an awards ceremony, or naming rights on a building. Do we consider that it's also going to a meeting down the block, listening, and asking questions? That it's allowing someone else to go before us in the grocery checkout line because they have a baby with them or look just plain tired? The process of honoring begins in the small gestures. Over a lifetime that becomes a life of honor.

Giving Others Permission to Change

"He always . . ." "She never . . ."

These absolutes assume we know how someone or something will respond in a given situation. And just as we approach truth with the ability and freedom to change our minds, we can offer those around us the ability to grow and change. If I were to treat Derek as the same person he was twenty years ago, that would not be fair to either of us. If I treated my eleven-year-old as if she were still two years old, my parenting would be ineffective and plain silly. People change. Sometimes we don't want them to change. It can cause hurt and disappointment and be disorienting. Sometimes we pray for them to make needed changes for their own thriving and the health of those around them.

Whether or not we are hoping someone will change, to honor the people around us, we need to offer them the freedom to grow and change. This recognizes the free will God has given each of us. If we want others to give us space to take in new information, form different opinions, and have a change of heart, we must offer the same flexibility to them. If we've already canceled someone because of some offense, we aren't giving them this freedom. This is different from setting healthy boundaries. If someone is harmful to us, it is good to set up parameters so the relationship isn't toxic. However, if we are simply dismissing the totality of a person, refusing to recognize their contributions because of a belief or behavior, we are creating systems of conditional relationships and limiting beliefs.

Here are a few things that help as we give others freedom to change and honor who they are as full people:

Eliminate absolutes. Words like *never, always,* and *typical* assume someone will stay a certain way indefinitely. They limit others' agency and box people into caricatures rather than vibrant, full individuals who

MAKING ROOM FOR CHANGE

Consider someone you would like to see make changes.
Ask yourself:

» What specifically do I want them to change? Is this
  about their beliefs or about their behaviors?

  _____

  _____

  _____

  _____

» What do I assume about them? Is this based on
  recent information? If not, how reliable are these
  assumptions?

  _____

  _____

  _____

  _____

» What do I know to be true of this person?

  _____

  _____

» Where have I seen growth in our relationship? How did that happen? Where could I intentionally cultivate growth?

sometimes do things well (according to our definitions) and sometimes don't.

Avoid assumptions. Of course, we use the information people have given us in the past to make informed decisions, but we can too easily branch into many assumptions from that known information. I know what it's like to have people make false assumptions about me based on given, true details of my life or worldview. It feels minimizing.

Lead with what is true. Thinking on what is noble or honorable about the person in front of you is going to place you in a mindset that first chooses to see the goodness in that person. We can always know they are made and loved by God. Leading with that knowledge greatly improves our odds of moving in the right direction.

Continually learn. Ask questions. Keep listening. You might be surprised to learn someone has changed their mind about something or changed their approach or behavior. We can fall back into assuming established patterns are a person's default. However, if we continue to be in relationship, we may be pleasantly surprised by someone's change.

Leading with Honor

I cohost a podcast with my lifelong friend Krista. Our audience is primarily women whose lives look a lot like ours: they are married, they have kids at home, but some of their kids are starting to leave the nest. We have guests on who we believe will enrich our conversations and bring helpful ideas and practical applications to our listeners. A few times our decision to host certain guests has resulted in criticism from our listeners. The complaints have rarely been about the content of the interview but rather about the guest's beliefs, behaviors, or statements in other places. We've understood listeners' concerns. A person's integrity in one place impacts their integrity elsewhere. We also know that no guest is above reproach (that whole human imperfection we all live in). When a publicist pitches a guest, our responsibility as hosts is to ask, Does this person have something beneficial and unique to offer our listeners? We produce our podcast to serve our listeners, after all.

To automatically dismiss someone because of one element of who they are would be participating in the cancel culture we are working hard to erase. In fact, we have five stated core values for our podcast, and one of them is unity. We are clear about what we believe and what we stand for. We also are building a large enough tent that we can hold differences of belief with some of our guests. And we can honor what they do add to the larger conversation by asking what they can uniquely bring that our listeners would value. This is honoring who our guests are and who our listeners are. Is it a foolproof system? Of course not. Do we sometimes get complaints anyway? Yes. Have we had a guest speaking on a topic that feels incongruous with their actual lives? I can think of only one.

When I received my slew of cancel messages for my Instagram post, I asked myself, *Who in the past has modeled healthy disagreement with me? Has anyone ever approached me in a way that felt uncomfortable (conflict, after all) but appropriate?* My friend Michelle came to mind. She had an issue with a guest we had on the podcast. She messaged me asking for a phone conversation. Her tone throughout the conversation was gentle. She expressed the value of our relationship and her respect for me, and she asked lots of questions about our decision-making process. I truly felt like she wanted to learn. She also asked me some difficult, pointed questions that made me consider with more depth our guest-selection process. It wasn't an easy or comfortable conversation, but it was a healthy one because it was founded on mutual respect. Michelle led with honor.

In a response to a recent email from a listener questioning our decision to have a particular guest on the show,

Krista avoided a defensive posture. Her response opened with what she appreciated about our listener's feedback.

> Thank you for your email. Both Alex and I have read it and we are so grateful you came to us directly with your question. We appreciate that so much. And we welcome discussion. It's actually one of our high values.

Krista then went on to reaffirm our stated values and beliefs. She didn't defend our decision to have this guest on (my instinctive response) but instead honored the listener's approach of coming to us directly to ask questions rather

QUESTIONS TO CONSIDER WHEN IDENTIFYING WHAT IS HONORABLE ABOUT A PERSON

» How does this person uniquely reflect God's character?

» What qualities did they display that can be celebrated?

» How did they change or grow for the better?

» What would Jesus say about them if he was standing here right now?

» What potential do I see in this person? How can I encourage growth in this area?

than immediately unfollowing or publicly spewing on the internet. Krista led with honor.

To lead with honor is, of course, the right thing to do. However, it also has some secondary benefits. It can prevent a potential conflict from erupting. It takes what could be used for harm and turns it into what can be used for good. Krista is good at asking, "What did this person do right or well? How can I both acknowledge and even celebrate it?"

Attacking Ideas, Not People

I was just starting to make dinner when the news came in on my phone that Supreme Court Justice Ruth Bader Ginsburg died. I'd anticipated an uneventful Friday evening with everyone home and no other plans than to watch TV and ease into the weekend. But when I heard the news that this woman who served our country for decades had passed, I had an urgent need to do something symbolic to honor her. Our American flag was my first thought. Hanging the flag would certainly be a gesture of respect. I got the flag out of our coat closet near the front door, stepped out onto the front porch, and placed the short pole in its holder.

A few minutes later as we were talking as a family about RBG's legacy, Derek said, "We should fly the flag at half-mast." The silence and puzzled expressions the girls and I offered showed our skepticism. We didn't have a flagpole, just a stick long enough to extend the flag off our porch. But Derek was adamant that this was the most honoring way to fly our flag. I followed him out onto the porch and watched him squish the flag down the short stick to make our own half-mast. It looked sloppy and a bit pathetic, but we thought it was perfect.

Our honoring process is rarely neat. It doesn't always have the polished feel we are going for. But when it is sincere and from the heart, it doesn't really matter that the fabric is scrunched and the flagpole is short.

Here's the other thing about that moment: neither Derek nor I agreed with all of RBG's rulings, opinions, or ideas. But we didn't have to agree with her to know she was a woman worth honoring. The debate in our house was not whether to honor her—she'd served our country with personal sacrifice and genuine good intentions—but rather whether anyone would recognize that our scrunched-up flag on a stick was meant to be an ode to this incredible woman. Justice Ginsburg was famous for many of the cases she argued and won as a civil rights attorney, for her prominence on the Supreme Court, and for her trailblazing nature from law school to the highest court. We wanted to recognize her service. Mining for the good was not difficult. And our honoring her was without hesitation because we knew it didn't have to mean total agreement.

Justice Ginsburg is also famous for her ongoing friendship with her fellow Supreme Court justice Antonin Scalia. Though the two often came to different conclusions in the courtroom, they had a mutual affection and trust that endured professional differences. At Justice Scalia's memorial service, Justice Ginsburg included this story in her eulogy:

> Once asked how we could be friends given our disagreement on lots of things, Justice Scalia answered, "I attack ideas, I don't attack people. Some very good people have some very

bad ideas. And if you can't separate the two you gotta get another day job. You don't want to be a judge, at least not a judge on a multi-member panel."[2]

The two justices' ongoing friendship and loyalty received much publicity because it went against today's common public mudslinging. It stood out in a world of sound bites, twenty-four-hour news cycles looking for the latest zinger to grab our diminishing attention spans, and the oversaturated media machine. Yet most of us have relationships with people with whom we hold deep disagreements. Often they are within our families. Because we can't choose who we are related to, it's in these God-ordained relationships that

HONORING OFTEN REQUIRES CREATIVITY

Live creatively, friends. If someone falls into sin, forgivingly restore him, saving your critical comments for yourself. You might be needing forgiveness before the day's out. (Gal. 6:1 MSG)

» Consider how you might live creatively when you feel the need to offer a critical comment.
» How can you honor a person's "good" when tempted to call out their "bad"?

we find both differences and affection. These relationships exist and continue independently of agreement on everything. We also find them in our workplaces, churches, and neighborhoods. People we care for are different from us. As Justice Scalia pointed out, we can separate the heart of a person from their ideas.

God Has Not Left Us: Bless and Release

Derek reminds me often to "bless and release." As I am baffled by someone's take that is different from mine, he reminds me that agreement is not required but blessing is. *But I thought we were so similar!* Here we go into my self-made categories: we have kids in the same grade, we are part of the same Sunday school class, we _____ [fill in the blank]. I assume because this person and I choose to live or believe the same in one way, we must live or believe the same in other given ways too. I want people to think like I do, come to the same conclusions I do, and believe like me. It affirms me and is more comfortable. It's also not always realistic.

When all else fails and I can't come to an agreement with someone, I choose to believe the best in them and to trust that God is working in both of us. In some ways this is how my friend Michelle and I ended our phone conversation. Talking it through made us both see a few key differences to our decision-making processes that brought us to different conclusions. Because of our depth of friendship, we could "bless and release" and stay in relationship. Sometimes that's not possible if the foundation isn't there or the differences are too hurtful. It may be time to "bless and release" here too so that we avoid the temptation to cut someone down and still believe God is working out his big story in all things.

When we choose honor, we are not only offering blessing and releasing the other person into the world to carry out God's purposes in the way they see fit; we are also releasing ourselves of the burden of having to police everyone around us. We can let God be in charge while we take responsibility for what is ours: to offer honor whenever and wherever possible. This will give us a better lens to find and see what is true and beautiful.

A Prayer for
WHATEVER IS NOBLE

At a time when people do not listen,
Do not respect,
Do not honor while disagreeing,
We ask for a better way.

In an era of news cycles
And partisan takes
And "othering" the unknown,
We yearn for mutual respect.

When the world shows its way and we know it's not your
way, Lord,
Give us the patience and discipline to choose your
rhythms over our immediate reactions.

May we be people who lead through gentleness
Even when our emotions run high,
Our sensibilities get offended,
And our heads shake with disbelief.

May we be people who remember the humanity of every
neighbor,
Offering mercy in grief,
Generosity in need,
And celebration at a job well done.

May we see others as you do:
As people reflecting the creative God that you are,
As sinners in need of the grace that you offer,
As wondrous, complicated, complex beings in need of
*   your love.*

It is in this countercultural way of honoring the best
*   parts of one another*
That we will be reminded of the good parts of you.

May we choose the way of honor over and over
Until we are reunited with you.

In Jesus's name we pray.

Amen.

QUESTIONS *for* REFLECTION

1. Have you been "canceled"? How did it feel?

2. What is the benefit of being with people who have different starting places? How do they help you seek out goodness?

3. How has someone held you accountable in a way that was honoring? How can you incorporate more of that approach into your life?

4. How are you giving others room to change and grow? How are others doing the same for you?

5. What is one area of your life or one relationship where you can work on leading with honor? How will you do that?

Permission to Change

Jordan was close to her grandfather. As a girl, she and her sister would go to his house during their mom's weekly evening Bible study. While her grandma worked the night shift, Jordan's grandpa would babysit and make his signature junk food dinners. As she grew, Jordan heard stories of her grandpa's Korean War adventures, tall tales for a short-statured man. She watched as he ran his small lawn-care business and admired the long hours he worked and his skilled green thumb that was able to make anything grow. She would also hear comments he made about men that he hired. They weren't intentionally mean-spirited, but they led to generalizations about Black men that fed his stereotypes.

When Jordan was in college, she brought her boyfriend (now husband), Marques, home to meet her family. Marques is Black. Jordan and her family are not. Jordan wasn't sure how her grandfather would react to her new love. Her mother wasn't sure either. Jordan was concerned but not deterred. She believed her grandfather could rise to the occasion.

Marques visited over Christmas break. All meet-the-parents moments can be nerve-racking, but this one had more specific layers of questions around acceptance.

As Jordan's grandfather got to know Marques, he found they had two things in common: a strong work ethic and a love for Jordan. The elder's preconceived ideas about Black men were now being replaced by a relationship with a real person who displayed the opposite of his assumptions. Jordan's grandfather was moving past some of his previous biases. All of this was happening while his heart was becoming generally more tender. His age, ill health, and openness to the gospel were all shaping him into a more affectionate and accepting man. He was changing.

Now as Jordan looks back at her grandfather's softening, she sees God's goodness at work. As he opened himself to God's love and acceptance, he was better able to articulate his affection for his wife, daughter, granddaughter, and grandson-in-law. This did not happen in a vacuum. The people around him knew they didn't see eye to eye with him on everything. Some of that was perhaps generational, a result of old habits or worldviews, and some was just ignorance from lack of experience. Instead of blaming and shaming her grandfather for his personal biases, Jordan and Marques presented him with the opportunity to do better, think better, and believe better. They gave him room and space to change while honoring the character traits they also valued: hard work and loyalty.

How might the story have looked different if Jordan had said to Marques, "You can't come meet my family. My grandfather would never accept you"? Or if she had said to her grandfather, "Never mind, we won't see you this Christmas," because she knew it might be uncomfortable? Instead, Jordan, her mother, and Marques made room for Jordan's grandfather to change because they honored him enough to believe his God-given free will could allow him to grow. And he did.

Part 3

CULTIVATING MORAL COURAGE

Whatever is right . . .

PHILIPPIANS 4:8

The time is always right to do what is right.

DR. MARTIN LUTHER KING JR.

J ust because you can, doesn't mean you should." How many times have I said this to my children? Much is permissible in this world, but just because it's allowed doesn't make it the best choice. When a new checkout line opens at the grocery store and the checker waves at us, the last people in line, she's technically inviting us to the front. But what about the woman who is ahead of us and has been waiting ten minutes longer? Just because we can saunter to the now-open register doesn't mean we should. A manager at a restaurant stops by our table and asks how the service has been. If we're honest, it hasn't been stellar. We could tell the manager that, or we could offer our hardworking server a break, recognizing he had three groups sit down at the same time. Just because we can complain doesn't mean we should. Often we can be technically correct but lacking in mercy and grace. Moral courage involves doing what is right, above what is permitted.

Honoring others by respectfully allowing them to share their ideas and opinions does not mean we are not to consider, verbalize, and act on our own. In fact, the world is crying out for Jesus-loving people to follow his lead and act on what is right. This may mean going against a peer group, family structure, or theological framework that has grown comfortable. We must be willing to examine our assumptions, do our research, and see where God is leading to decide what he wants from us individually and corporately. Jesus did not automatically side with the norms of his day but exhibited the moral courage to do and say what he believed to be most God honoring. It is not tidy work but sometimes gut-wrenching, courageous work, where we step into difficult places as stewards of the gospel for our generation. Establishing moral courage is to know when it is right to say something and when it is more right not to.

Some translations of Philippians 4:8 replace the word *right* with *just* or *reputable*. The Greek word *díkaios* means "righteous," to be faultless or acceptable of God, but it can also mean giving people or processes what they are due.[1] When we consider what is right or just, we should be thinking in terms of God's kingdom. And his kingdom works in upside-down ways. After telling the parable of the workers in the vineyard, Jesus said, "So the last will be first, and the first will be last" (Matt. 20:16). His words inform what is right, just, and even reputable. We ask God to give us eyes to see with this upside-down lens what is right, and then we follow his lead regardless of whether it's comfortable or convenient.

But how does developing moral courage help us see goodness in the world? It sounds difficult with lots of potential conflict involved. When we are thinking on what is right or just, we are considering how God is already moving in the world. His movement is good! Creation. Separation. Reconciliation. Redemption. I picture a tide—a force of how God is making changes, establishing his kingdom already—and joining it. We're jumping on the wave of his movement and making our small contribution toward goodness. We take those ideas of what is true and honorable and expand them to action so that we are reflecting God's upside-down kingdom.

Right Thinking Leads to Right Living

"I'll pay anyone twenty dollars to memorize the Lord's Prayer and Psalm 23."

Our family of six was sitting around the dinner table, having a conversation about the lost art of memorization, and Derek threw out a challenge with a clear reward.

One girl spoke for the crowd. "I don't understand why we can't just Google it when we need it."

Our daughters are obviously of the digital generation, and they had a point. We can now search for anything at any time and get an answer of some kind. But there is something about truth being woven into our minds and hearts to call on if ever we need it. We talked about prisoners of war and how they've depended on Scripture memorized as a child to carry them through horrific situations. Apparently none of our girls plan to be prisoners of war, so the example didn't quite convince them. We resorted to the trusted parenting approach—bribery. We used what was important to them: cold, hard cash. Perhaps not the purest motive (that's part 4) but an end result we could all agree on (see "Different Starting Places" from part 2).

I considered how many times the words "Give us this day our daily bread" had popped into my head in the last few years. In a time when it has felt impossible to count on anything—income, health, plans—I've had to ask God to give me what I need for today. I had those words from the Lord's Prayer to recall because they were embedded in my brain. I could then quickly remind my heart and mind of what they say when I felt afraid.

Over and over I've stood at the sink washing dishes, remembering that God has answered my prayer to give me what I need for today. *"Give us this day our daily bread." Thank you, Lord, for today's supply. Food in the cupboards, patience (mostly) for my children, a husband who repeatedly shows up in the middle of the drudgery and the stress. I have what I need.* The prayer is there to remind me and helps me move on to the next task of the moment for the day. He gave me what I needed, so my job is to do what is required of me. Just for today. He has given me my portion even though I tend to get ahead of myself and him. Those words bring me back to the moment and ask me to take responsibility with the bread he has provided. Then off I go to make that hard phone call or pay the bills I've been avoiding, because right thinking leads to right living.

Our minds are meant to settle on things that are different from what our news feeds, our social media feeds, or even our self-talk offer. We do things like memorize Scripture so we have something good within us to draw from. Romans 12:2 says, "Do not conform to the pattern of this world, but be transformed by the renewing of your mind." When I marinate in the things that are right, my mind changes.

As our understanding of the brain grows, we find this concept of renewing the mind is confirmed by science. The way and the frequency with which we think about things impacts our behaviors. When we process only what is stressful and bad, we lose the ability to think quickly or be creative. The more we focus on the negative, the more synapses and neurons are created in those familiar ruts, which push us back to a negative thought process.[2] In other words, we create patterns reinforcing that we see what we're looking for. The more we seek out goodness and the more we look for the positive, the easier it will be for our brains to identify what is good.

The promise after Philippians 4:8 is that if we fill our minds with the things of God's goodness, we will have peace. Eugene Peterson paraphrased Philippians 4:9 in The Message: "Put into practice what you learned from me, what you heard and saw and realized. Do that, and God, who makes everything work together, will work you into his most excellent harmonies." Well, that sounds delightful and like all the things I want—to be in God's most excellent harmonies. Thinking on the things God tells us to leads to good

SETTING OUR MINDS ON WHAT IS RIGHT

Memorize the Lord's Prayer (Matt. 6:9–13) or Psalm 23. (There will be no twenty-dollar bill coming your way unless you work that out with your own dad.)

practice, the kind of practice that puts us in harmony with his work in this world. That sounds like we are moving toward what is right and just and good.

A Kingdom Perspective

The Lord's Prayer is Jesus's example of how to pray. It is not lost on me that it includes "your kingdom come, your will be done, on earth as it is in heaven" (Matt. 6:10). Jesus talked about the kingdom of God as a present and current state, right in our midst. It's something we have access to.

> Jesus, grilled by the Pharisees on when the kingdom of God would come, answered, "The kingdom of God doesn't come by counting the days on the calendar. Nor when someone says, 'Look here!' or, 'There it is!' And why? Because God's kingdom is already among you." (Luke 17:20–21 MSG)

Here is the beautiful thing about God's kingdom: it is the process of making things right in all the places where the world is not as it should be. It is the process of redemption and reconciliation in every corner of the world. So when we look for what is right and find it, we are guaranteed to see God's goodness at work.

Derek works at Providence Network, a ministry where people live together in community. Many of them are working on sobriety, some have recently left violent and toxic relationships, and others are getting their mental health back to where it should be. It is meant to be a place of healing, of resting in God's goodness and accepting his grace. This is true for those who are on staff and those who are receiving services. Is it peaceful? Sometimes. Seamless? Never. Is it a demonstration of God's kingdom here on earth? Yes, because it tells the gospel story—of creation, separation, reconciliation, and redemption—in the details of people's lives. This is a story that is told over and over. It is told in a moment of choosing exercise over substance. It is told in a year of therapy and slow growth. It is told in a lifetime, as we all aim to move in the general direction of God's grace and mercy.

We can see God's kingdom when we ask, What is right? What is just? As with all things, sometimes it is easier to see the opposite of what we are searching for in order to see where God is at work, to see the light because of the darkness. Injustice hits our spirits in a way that brings pause. We feel the disconnect between what should be and what actually is. It is our God-given wiring that sounds the alarms: this is not the way the world is supposed to work. My children proclaim that sentiment with "It's not fair" or "That's not right." Our more mature sensibilities might look at it as "It's not just" or "People deserve better." To see goodness at work is to see the unjust made right. It does not look like what is lovely or pure, but it also isn't that far removed. When God's kingdom comes, we see things that are beautiful. The lovely, pure, and just overlap in a Venn diagram of goodness.

Seeing the unjust at Providence Network helps me to see God's goodness. The light in contrast to the darkness. Is it right for a woman to have to sneak her children out of their home to escape an abuser? Obviously not. Is it right for someone to offer them a safe place to land? Obviously it is.

A number of years ago I interviewed a woman. Let's call her Cindy. She was living at Providence Network with her two young daughters, and we were taping her story to be shared at a fundraising event to give the audience a sense of what residents were leaving behind when they came to "Prov." Cindy described a life of terror—her boyfriend threatening her physical safety, not letting her leave the house without his permission. Control, abuse of power, and physical harm defined their relationship. She wasn't sure what had kept her with him. Maybe it was the financial support—she'd be homeless if she left—maybe it was the belief that she was being treated as she deserved, or maybe it was simply what was familiar. Cindy was sure, however, of what motivated her to finally leave. Her boyfriend hit one of the girls. Suddenly her need to protect her children became more important than any of her reasons to stay with him. The next day while her boyfriend was at work, Cindy packed a few bags, and she and her girls left.

How do we see what was just or right here? The foreboding story is one of manipulation, anger gone wrong, and malice. It is the vulnerable being kicked while they are down both figuratively and literally. It is the antithesis of goodness. As far as I know, this man was never charged with any crimes; the courts did not seek justice on the victims' behalf. He was not punished in any way here on earth other than being left alone to his own conscience. Where is the goodness here?

The goodness was in Cindy's courage, in her determination to take steps she never thought possible because she loved her children enough to face the fear of life without a man. It was in the temporary shelter that took them in and arranged for their longer-term housing at Providence Network. It was in her new home and community of women and children with similar stories—those who stepped over and through their old belief systems to get to a new and better place, both in home and in heart. It was in the staff that lived just down the hall from Cindy and her girls, because this community wasn't about shift work but about re-creating family with new norms of operating, ones filled with love and hope. It was even in the audience of financial supporters who were going to hear her words and were asking, *Lord, how can I help? Where do I fit?*

Creation. Separation. Reconciliation. Redemption. The pattern was evident in Cindy's story. It wasn't done, as in all wrapped up and tied with a bow. This side of heaven we will always be working toward restoring what is right. But that's just it—we don't have to wait for heaven to experience God's kingdom. We hold the tension as we search for goodness, seeing the wrong made right while knowing we will always live within a world that aches.

AN EXERCISE IN CONSIDERING
WHAT IS RIGHT

Think of one situation where you have been wronged.

》 Where was Jesus during your frustration, pain, or anger?

》 How did Jesus use other people to be messengers of hope to you?

》 Were you surprised by how Jesus made things right? If so, how?

Taking Time to Consider What Is Right

Remember when I got canceled? When the mean-spirited messages started rolling in, I was a bit in shock, and then my feelings came. I needed to wait a few hours, a few days, to decide the right way to respond.

In an era of tweets and out-of-context quotes and raging opinions, we can feel the pressure to say something publicly about the issue of the moment. We are used to immediate responses. We text someone and wonder why they aren't texting back. We are a culture of the urgent. Our shortened attention spans play into this, and we begin to think instant is the norm. We forget that God makes seasons change gradually over months, that he takes nine months to grow a baby, and that he makes generations wait in the desert before he leads them out. We all know through our own desperate prayers that God's timing is often slower, his message often quieter, and his goodness often subtler than we are accustomed to.

For this reason it is okay to slow down, pray, consider where God's goodness is evident, and refrain from making immediate declarations or statements. This is especially difficult when silence can be interpreted as apathy, compliance, support, or disagreement. In other words, silence can be heard as many different things. If we don't say something, how will people know how we feel? The simple answer is they won't, and that's okay. Sometimes we don't know what is right, and we must take the time to determine it. We've all seen the fallout of jumping quickly to conclusions about who has been wronged and who is at fault. It's as if almost every week there is a news story around an "unjust" moment and a week later a follow-up story on the context that gives us a broader understanding.

We're reminded in the book of James, "My dear brothers and sisters, take note of this: Everyone should be quick to listen, slow to speak and slow to become angry" (1:19). As we consider what is right, we can follow these three steps: listen, hold our tongues, and get a handle on our emotions. We will then be better able to see where God is already at work and decide how we are best able to join him in that work. We are people who are looking for a broader understanding of what is going on in the world. We can't have God's perspective, but we can slow ourselves down enough to step in that direction.

This does not mean we are to wait when there is an emergency. There are times to speak *now* because there is an urgency that can't be ignored. In those moments, we say what needs to be said because danger needs to be averted. Then we step back to implement the three steps of listening, holding our tongues, and getting a handle on our emotions in order to find God's goodness.

But how do we know if something is right or just? How do we see the good in very unjust situations? We ask some questions (being quick to listen), pray (being slow to speak), and consider how the arc of Scripture informs us (being slow to anger).

It can be difficult to set aside space in your life to consider what is right or just. Here are a few practices that can help you be more intentional:

Slow down. You don't want to say or do something you might later regret. Give yourself the freedom not to

make a call or decision for a set amount of time—
twenty-four hours, a week. This will help your emotions settle so you can think with more clarity.

Seek out varied voices. Are there multiple viewpoints
on what you are considering? Are you listening to
them? God gave you a discerning mind. Don't be
afraid to listen to different perspectives as you determine what is just.

Look to Scripture. God's Word is given to all people for
all time. The stories are relevant to questions of justice today. Look for both themes and direct instruction on how you are to behave and engage with the
world as a Christ follower.

QUESTIONS TO CONSIDER WHEN DETERMINING HOW TO MOVE FORWARD

» What would make things more just or right, given
God's upside-down kingdom?
» How is God already working to make things right?
How can I join him?
» How am I uniquely positioned to move things
toward justice?
» Do my offerings of time, treasure, or talent help
or hinder the people they are intended to benefit?
How?

Pray. God, the source of knowledge and truth, is available to us in prayer. Ask him to give you needed information, wisdom, insight, and eyes to see the world as he sees it. Ask the Holy Spirit to guide you as you discern what is right.

Articulate. With complicated issues we often form ideas over time. As we begin to articulate our thinking, we see where wrong thinking (ours and others') might be taking place. Journal, talk it out with a trusted friend, or just pray out loud so you are privately putting words to your thoughts before speaking them publicly with haste.

Confirm. Once you think you understand what is right or just, consider how it fits into the arc of grace. Creation. Separation. Reconciliation. Redemption. Justice can often be understood within this larger pattern.

Once we feel we know what is right, it's time to decide if we're going to act. The process of discernment takes us back to thinking on what is true. When we feel overwhelmed about what is the right or just move to make, we can go back to the question, What do I know to be true of this situation? When we establish what we know to be true, we can then move toward what is morally right and what God requires of us. This process is thinking on what is right or just. The next question after thinking on these things is, What should I do with them?

"Just" Is Not the Same as "Fair"

My friend Lori once described a mutual friend as a person who gives people what they need rather than what they ask for. "It's very Christlike, really," Lori said. "Someone will ask her something, and rather than answering their specific question, she'll give them what their heart needs to hear." I've come back to that description many times when thinking about what is right or just.

As a parent, I can certainly understand the concept of someone thinking they need something from me when really they want something, and what they actually need goes deeper. As a parent, I also understand that what is "fair" is not always just.

Let's say I have two children. One has no problem with academics while the other has a learning disability and needs professional tutoring. In the concept of fairness, where everyone gets the same amount of everything, either both of my children or neither of them would get a tutor. We know that is ridiculous because only one needs the help, so to pay for a tutor for the student who is doing fine would be a waste of resources and to withhold tutoring from the one in need would be neglectful. Yet the amount spent on tutoring would be the same, or fair.

However, if we are looking for what is just in this situation, the child who needs the help would receive exactly what is needed, and the one already thriving will keep on doing what has worked for them. God's grace works in just the same way. The story of the prodigal son reminds us that God welcomes us home regardless of how long we've been gone or even if we've not been gone at all. His grace does not discriminate based on offense. The cross is not fair in that Jesus's sacrifice was not what *he* deserved, but it is right. He gives me my daily bread whether I'm just a little hungry or ravenous. Jesus gave us—and continues to give us—what

CONSIDER WHAT YOU NEED

» Sit with Jesus for a moment and consider what you want.

» Ask him for it. He wants to hear from you.

» Now ask him to reveal what you might need. Listen and wait.

» Observe as you move through your day how he is offering you daily bread.

we need, not what we ask for. It takes moral courage to ask him for what we need.

Peacemaking

When I think of working toward what is just or right, I think of a courtroom scene in a TV drama with a stellar closing argument by the prosecuting attorney and the bad guy or gal getting what he or she deserves. Or I think of an activist on the front lines protesting the injustice of the moment. I think of a battle with a good side and a bad side. This kind of tension doesn't exactly make me think of peace. And yet two things can be true at once. The way of making things right can be about making peace, and there can be a rub between the way things are and the way things are supposed to be.

There is a difference between peacekeeping and peace-making. As a parent, I've done my fair share of peace-keeping—for example, I try to keep everyone happy enough so there aren't fights in the back seat while I'm driving. I preemptively take measures to prevent conflict before it happens. I determine who sits next to whom in the car and in which rows of seats and what music we play as we're driving. I anticipate who will complain about what, and I make decisions accordingly to prevent the conflict from bubbling to the surface. This may sidestep some potential bickering, but it never gets to the heart of the matter: that my children must learn to be content in their circumstances. Not only that, but it is also exhausting trying to make everyone happy all the time.

Peacemaking, on the other hand, is about restoration. There may be conflict as part of the process, but the end goal is about working toward God's kingdom.

If I can settle myself enough in a heated moment to remember that peacemaking is my goal, I ask, *What is the way of Jesus? Where would he be in this situation? Who would he be facing? Where would he be standing? What would he be giving us that we need?* Those questions lead me closer to the heart of Christ, the very definition of what is true and beautiful, and from there I can make decisions on actions to take.

I had some hurt feelings when I got canceled. I was a bit bruised. But I also wanted to do right by people even if they hadn't done right by me. The idea of what is true and honorable feeds right into what is just. Part of what I said in response to one of my friends: "This doesn't feel like our relationship to me. One where we believe the best in each other and have an honest curiosity and respect when we don't understand. . . . In my experience this is not how friends respond to each other. I feel disoriented and unclear what you want from me." I wanted to defend myself against the assumptions she'd made and the anger she'd thrown my direction, but when I considered where Jesus would be standing and how he would be facing us, I knew he loved this woman even more than I did. I wanted to honor her. I wanted to be a peacemaker.

In *Common Prayer*, Shane Claiborne and Jonathan Wilson-Hartgrove say,

> Peacemaking doesn't mean passivity. It is the act of interrupting injustice without mirroring injustice, the act of disarming evil without destroying the evildoer, the act of finding a third way that is neither fight nor flight but the careful, arduous pursuit of reconciliation and justice. It is about a revolution of love that is big enough to set both the oppressed and the oppressors free. Peacemaking is about being able to recognize in the face of the oppressed our own faces, and in the hands of the oppressors our own hands.[3]

I wanted to disarm evil without destroying my friend. Instead of shutting the conversation down, I tried to be honest about my feelings while getting to the heart of hers. After some messages back and forth, she said, "THANK YOU for your grace and your forgiveness and this disconfirming experience. That I can screw it up and not be harmed, punished, or abandoned. But seen and loved." Doing what is just or right can involve natural consequences but shouldn't involve revenge. In God's kingdom, people are given another chance to do well. We can think on what that means and then extend the grace that Christ has offered us. I had to push back against my own defensiveness and ask myself, *What does peacemaking look like?* We have a choice to reflect God's goodness back to the world, participating in his big story of reconciliation and redemption.

Someone Has to Go First

Back to the downtown art museum trip in part 1 of this book. It was a hot summer day, but the dark room and the air-conditioning encouraged us to walk slowly through the exhibit. We wanted to linger to take in the paintings, some of them familiar because of their renown, and to enjoy the cooler air inside. We were visiting a temporary Norman Rockwell exhibit. His illustrations included details that told complex stories—a sailor's tattoo, a child's wailing face, a soda jerk's smirk. A nation's experience through a particular time period, told through the eyes of one artist. Rockwell was a man who mined for goodness as he observed his neighbors and reflected their experiences back to his fellow citizens.

We found ourselves—me and four girls who weren't even up to my shoulders yet—standing in front of a painting of another little girl. Her braids swung as she walked, books in hand. She wore a white dress with puffy short sleeves and white ankle socks and shoes. Two men in suits walked ahead of her, and two behind. A racial slur was painted on the wall they were walking alongside, with a tomato splatter dripping down the plaster. The squished tomato lying on the ground under the stained wall suggested a crime scene of a more violent nature. The painting was titled *The Problem We All Live With.*

111

There she was, Ruby Bridges, the six-year-old who was escorted by federal marshals to integrate an elementary school in New Orleans. It did not escape me that I had four little girls with me. That this history was only ten years before my arrival here on earth. That this girl was a first in her world at much personal cost—the first student of color to attend William Frantz Elementary School. The tomatoes and racial slur in the painting were signs of the very real threats to physical safety she faced, the men in suits a reminder that she needed protection the remainder of the year.

My next thought was of her parents. They had the courage to go first. Six-year-old Ruby would surely have had a more pleasant first-grade year had she stayed at her old school. She likely would have been able to better focus on her ABCs and 123s without the distraction of a mob screaming at her as she entered the building. Her parents had an opportunity to step forward and do their part to make an unjust system right but at great personal cost.

Looking at the painting, I thought, *Would I? Would I have had the moral courage to make such a dangerous move? One that would impact not only my child but our entire family? What were the conversations that happened around their dinner table as they weighed the options?* Seeing little Ruby's resolve portrayed in that painting and in the room's special exhibit dedicated to her story, I remembered that many people before me have chosen to go first. That requires a certain level of resolve in what is right. Remembering this helps us see goodness in a tangible way and inspires me to consider my own moral courage and ask where I might be called to step forward or even go first.

What Is Right Is Costly

It is in our nature to want to do what is easy and comfortable. Human nature is geared toward self-preservation. Cultural values of pleasure, comfort, and following our desires are not only permitted but they are also encouraged. And yet as Christians, we live in the upside-down world of "your kingdom come, your will be done, on earth as it is in heaven." I'm not saying God doesn't want us to enjoy life. Quite the opposite. The book of Ecclesiastes says, "I know that there is nothing better for people than to be happy and to do good while they live. That each of them may eat and drink, and find satisfaction in all their toil—this is the gift of God" (3:12–13). At the same time, Jesus said,

> If anyone would come after me, let him deny himself and take up his cross and follow me. For whoever would save his life will lose it, but whoever loses his life for my sake will find it. For what will it profit a man if he gains the whole world and forfeits his soul? Or what shall a man give in return for his soul? (Matt. 16:24–26 ESV)

Jesus was not joking around. He knew his mission here on earth was the opposite of comfort. He challenged religious legalism and pushed against those abusing power, especially those doing it in God's name. Ultimately he took on a painful death so that we all may live. He's not asking us to come close to his personal cost. He took on the sins of humanity, after all. He may be asking us to share our wealth, sit with a neighbor while our to-do list is put on hold, or ask uncomfortable questions of those in power. Those are actions within our reach and scope of influence.

113

Here is the rub of the Christian life. God tells us to enjoy what he gives us, this one life with all its blessings. Yet he says our life is not our own and we must be obedient when the time comes to do the good work of the kingdom. Though we are meant to give thanks for the extras (read: the comforts) given to us by our good Father, we are also to remember that the essentials to this life are found in him and who he is. If we make our comfort the center of our existence, the motivation behind our daily agenda, then we are at risk of missing the point of life: to love God and neighbor.

To do what is just or right is often our part of taking up the cross, of looking around and recognizing God has uniquely placed us in the moment, right where we are, to do something that reorders things back to God's purposes. We see where God is already working through creation, separation, reconciliation, and redemption, and we decide how we can contribute to his work.

Anything of value has a price. It costs us something. The more we work toward what is important in this world, the more costly it may be to us. At the same time the important work can have a higher reward. Thinking on what is just leads us to right living, which costs us time, money, and energy. Right living is costly and it is good.

God Has Not Left Us: We Don't Look Away

My friend Gena recently said, "Sometimes the Good News is bad news." Sometimes following Jesus requires us to give up some of our comforts, do something hard, and bear one another's burdens in a way that is painful. If we determine that what is good and right requires our action, it's time for a bit of moral courage. Following Christ comes at a cost that is minuscule in comparison to what we receive in return. He has blown breath into our lungs, makes the sun rise, and is the source of any good gifts we enjoy. He also asks us to think with a kingdom mindset and then follow his instruction.

There is a jump required from thinking on things that are right to acting on them. Sometimes the jump feels small, gentle, and easy. Other times it feels like a leap of faith across the Grand Canyon, and we're not sure we're going to make it. But when we think on what is right, we know in our spirits we must try to work toward what is just.

Gena and I met on the trip to the Texas-Mexico border I mentioned in part 2. It was a gut-wrenching few days, because we saw firsthand how things are not as they should be. People who fled violence in Central America arrived at the US border only to find themselves in different dangerous situations. We saw children held in cyclone-fencing "cages" and talked with teenage girls detained in prison-like facilities, waiting for asylum hearings. It was easy to see that things were not right, but we also quickly understood that the problems are tangled and complex. There were no easy solutions. We had new information and knew that lives were at risk and fellow image bearers were suffering. As a group of Christian authors, we knew we didn't have solutions that experts hadn't already considered. We also knew we couldn't look away. We couldn't unsee what we saw. We couldn't pretend away what we now knew.

We thought on what was right, we considered what God might be asking of us, and we returned home. I didn't feel

I had a clear answer to the question of how I could contribute to the solution, so I prayed a simple prayer: *Lord, I'm available.* For what, I wasn't sure, but I hoped he could use me, and I've committed to saying yes if my voice is in any way helpful to make right what is wrong in our immigration system. I've since traveled to DC to meet with lawmakers, and I've written a few nationally syndicated articles. When the opportunity has presented itself, I've said yes.

In some ways that trip to the border resulted in some of the most heartbreaking days of my life. In other ways it was hopeful because I saw other Christ followers asking the questions and being willing to work regardless of the cost. God's goodness is evident in the sacrificial, loving response to make wrong things right.

So when Gena says, "Sometimes the Good News is bad news," of course it is a bit tongue-in-cheek. The Good News of the gospel is always good. We are always glad to know that Christ is God incarnate who came to reconcile and draw us back to him. It's the "your kingdom come, your will be done, on earth as it is in heaven" part that can get a little painful because it requires moral courage. We can find that courage, knowing that God is with us, that he loves us, and that he is working through his big story of creation, separation, reconciliation, and redemption. Thinking on and working toward what is right might be hard, but that doesn't mean it's not good.

A Prayer for
WHATEVER IS RIGHT

We are quick to pray, "Your kingdom come,
  Your will be done,
  On earth as it is in heaven."
We say the words without considering the cost.
We want the kingdom without building the walls.
For this, Lord, forgive us.

And while we are asking for forgiveness,
Show us your mercy
  For the ways we've overlooked the needs of our
    neighbors,
  For the ways we've excused bad behavior, both ours
    and others', because it was easier,
  For the ways we've pretended that what was familiar
    was right.

Jesus, we have not walked in your way
When we've held back forgiveness,
When we've thought the cost too high to choose your
    kingdom,
When we've let fear be the dominant voice even though
    we've known you are asking us to rise in courage.
For these things, we are not proud.

Lord, we want to think on things that are right.
But first we must
   See the holes in systems,
   Examine our hearts and our motives,
   And acknowledge our part in the undoing.

Second we must
   Ask where your creation is hurting,
   Wonder how you might be making a way,
   And listen for your Spirit's prompting.

Third we must
   Take up the cross in front of us,
   Not because it is trendy or will gain us favor in this
      world
   But because it is your way.
And your way is not only better, it is best.

Lord, we pray again, "Your kingdom come,
   Your will be done,
   On earth as it is in heaven."
May we think on what this means right around us and
   serve you in ways that are easy and hard.

For yours is the kingdom and the power and the glory
   forever and ever.

Amen.

QUESTIONS *for* REFLECTION

1. Where can you work on right thinking? How might training your mind help you see God's kingdom with new eyes?

2. How have you experienced the difference between peacekeeping and peacemaking? How does peacemaking help you find what is just?

3. When have you asked Jesus for something you've wanted and received something you've needed instead? How was what he offered true and beautiful or even better than what you asked for?

4. When have you witnessed making things right at great personal cost? How has this reflected God's goodness to you?

5. Who might you be called to forgive? Where does that fit into what is right?

The Cost of Doing What's Right

"We have learned the practice of letting go of the good for the sake of the best." My friend Rachel was describing the impact being a foster parent has had on her family life. Rachel and her husband, James, have two young biological children, and with the ebb and flow of what is foster parenting, they have additional kids join their family for a season. Sometimes it's a single child, other times it's a sibling pair. Some have stayed a weekend as a respite for other foster families, others have stayed months. To say it is disruptive to their lives would be an understatement. Rachel has passed on professional opportunities and hasn't volunteered in her oldest daughter's classrooms like she thought she would. She and James have lost friendships because of the time and energy involved with foster parenting. Welcoming foster children into their home has impacted every detail of daily life.

When Rachel and James first considered foster care, they were experiencing secondary infertility. They had been trying for years to get pregnant again and then miscarried twins. They saw foster care as a potential road toward adoption. Rachel told me, "During our first weekend of training, it became abundantly clear to us that fostering with the sole intention of growing our family was not what God was calling us to. Foster care is about loving and caring for a child or children with the hope of reunification with their family. Our story has also been of walking alongside biological family members as they work to put their lives back together. And while we are open to adoption should reunification not be possible, that hasn't been the path God has chosen for us as of yet."

This is not a life of glamour. There is no reality show following them around. There are no crowds to witness their sacrifice. There is simple daily task after daily task of making breakfast, doing dishes, going on walks, and playing board games. There is also comforting in the middle of the night, receiving pushback on new boundaries, and attending lots of court and therapy appointments. There is the cost of time, attention, and energy. There is the difficult part of saying goodbye and helping their two biological daughters transition away from what becomes a new normal with other kids in the home. This is a real grief, but one they know is part of the good. As Rachel said, "It is letting go of the good for the sake of the best."

There is also the benefit of witnessing growth and receiving affection and gentle surprises that remind them the work is holy. One of the biggest surprises for Rachel and James has been the hope and hard work they have seen in the parents working to be reunited with their children. The parents of the first children they fostered gave them new insights and new information that helped them see why and how a family was in this spot in the first place. Rachel said, "These weren't *evil* people who had intentionally given up their children. Sure, they had made bad choices and often acted selfishly—but I do that sometimes too. They were hurting parents stuck in a cycle of addiction without God or any kind of support system to help them make a change. I realized then that my husband and I, as foster parents, could also be an encouragement, support, and vessel of Christ's love to the children in our home as well as their parents." Rachel and James's attempt to seek out goodness for the sake of foster children led them to seek out goodness for the entire family.

Foster parenting has not been about making Rachel and James feel good about themselves. There is lots of heartache and hard work involved. It is certainly not about being the hero in anyone else's story. It is about supporting a foster child during a temporary crisis and cheering for the biological parents as they make changes that will stabilize their lives enough that the child can be safely reunited with them. It is knowing that God's kingdom works toward reconciliation and redemption whenever possible. Rachel and James can't right the exact wrongs these children have suffered, but they can do their part to restore structure, safety, and security to one or two people at a time as their family of origin gets stabilized. This is a commitment to do what is right within their scope of influence, even when it comes at great personal cost. It is about letting go of the good for the sake of the best.

Part 4

THE FRUIT IS GOOD

Whatever is pure . . .

PHILIPPIANS 4:8

Faith is holding on tight when the going gets windy.

CHARLES SCHULTZ

Linda held out a plastic tub, a yogurt container now repurposed for our morning berry harvest. Though it had been years, I felt like it was just yesterday that she was handing me a bucket and scooting me out of her door to her garden. My mom, my older two girls, and I were on a visit to the island outside of Seattle where I'd spent a few of my earliest years. We were staying with dear friends who have always been like family to us. The berry buckets, walking to the large, fenced garden, the blue July sky of the Pacific Northwest, and the chickens in their pen felt like whispers from my childhood in this special spot. My city girls were not used to being sent outside to harvest for the breakfast spread. We picked more raspberries than we could eat. They were ripe and ready and oh so good as we sampled a few while still standing next to the bush. The warm berries tasted like pure summer, and it was nothing but good.

Very little in this world is pure. This side of heaven, we live in a mixed-up space of God's holiness and humanity's fall. Every relationship, person, or system is flawed because we live in a broken world, but that does not mean that God is not present in those places. Quite the contrary—he is in all those places. Our job is to find where he is at work and call it out. It is the mining process that requires prayer, study (to know God's character), and the willingness to find him in unexpected ways. We know that the fruit of the Spirit is what is evident in our lives as the Holy Spirit does this work in us. Love, joy, peace, patience, kindness, goodness, faithfulness, gentleness, and self-control (Gal. 5:22–23) are good because they are the result of God's work. The fresh raspberries were delicious, and the fruit of the Spirit is a delight to taste. It is flavorful and nutritious. The fruit is good.

When I think of the raspberries straight from the bush, I know that God makes good things. He is the original organic farmer. He created the elements on the periodic table in their pure form. He is the source of pure love and pure joy. So though very little in this world is pure, when we find hints of purity, we can celebrate it with raucous cheers.

A baby's first steps may be wobbly, but they are an indication of so much pure good in God's creation. Life and growth are evident in those unsteady moves. They might not be perfect, but like the child leaning toward a parent's open arms, they are steps headed in the right direction. We can keep this mindset as we look for what is pure and good.

The Message paraphrases *pure* in Philippians 4:8 as "authentic." In a time when authenticity is valued, we can ask what it means to think on what is authentic. Sometimes *authentic* is skewed to mean that which is messy, honest, even rude. "I'm just being honest" can be a cover-up for what is truly mean-spirited. No, *authentic* gets back to what is true. In this life we live, where we hold joy and pain simultaneously, authenticity is recognizing these two tensions coexist. To see only the joy without the pain is not the authentic life. So as we search for what is pure, we know this side of glory we are always holding the authentic, which is the reality of God's pure goodness in the midst of his big story that is still in process. A pure faith is an authentic one.

Another way to look at what is pure is to look for where there is hope. Jesus is the hope of the world. If we look for places that point toward the possibility of what can be through him, we are seeking what is pure in the midst of a messy life. We are seeking out what is good.

Finite Disappointment versus Infinite Hope

My two youngest girls and I parked at a familiar neighborhood intersection with an anticipation of normal. This was the first activity we'd signed up for pre–COVID shutdown that had not been canceled. What could hold such anticipation? Two girls' dentist appointments. It's not that we were excited about the dentist; in fact, they had their typical nerves. It's that it felt "normal." Like things we used to do. We had masks with us, knowing we'd likely need to be wearing them in the office when the girls' mouths weren't wide open for others to peer in. We put them on as we stood on the corner across the street from the brick city building. We could see another masked family standing outside the door, which suggested there was a new system in place to go in. We'd been so few places outside of the grocery store and occasional Target run that we were automatically struck by how this "routine" visit was not going to be routine.

We crossed the street and read the sign taped to the door. We were to text that we'd arrived and then wait to be let in, where we'd all be screened with temperature checks. There was resolve—*Okay, we'll make the best of this*—but what my two girls didn't know was that I'd spent the morning canceling our summer vacation. Not our original vacation, mind you. That had been canceled months earlier. No, this was the plan B that was getting canceled. Both were out-of-state trips (the first by air, the second by car, because we were no dummies and were going to make the classic American road trip work for us), but both destination states had declared fourteen-day self-quarantines for out-of-state guests after our reservations were made. The disappointment was there.

I can recognize when my hurt comes from my privilege. To mourn a canceled vacation means life's baseline is pretty good to start with. But it was the only thing we had. All public pools in our city and surrounding cities—closed. Overnight camp—canceled. Summer jobs for the older girls—impossible with the risks. It felt like these dentist appointments were the only thing normal in our schedule, and even here we were hit with how different the world was.

I felt defeated. Even though it was only midmorning, the heat from the sidewalk was pushing up toward us. We tried to peer through the windows to see if there was any indication how things inside were unfolding, but the glare and the tint to keep the intense Colorado sun out kept us from seeing in. Our eyes focused instead on the construction-paper flowers taped to the glass as decorations, with inspirational quotes written in the centers. My inner cynic thought a few lighthearted quotes were meant to appease us as the sweat dripped down our backs and our lives were turned upside down. But then I noticed one of the quotes was from Bob Ross, a TV painter sporting the most amazing blossoming hair. Just thinking of him and the possibility that he might be an inspirational thought leader made me smile.

> Anytime you learn, you gain.
>
> —Bob Ross

Well, Bob, sometimes I don't want to learn. Some life lessons don't contribute to my inner growth or inner hope. I like Bob, but he wasn't really inspiring me. The critic was done with the inspiration offered by the dentist's office staff. I wanted to move on to the routine part of this appointment.

And then my eyes focused in on words written on a white cloud at the end of a construction-paper rainbow.

You may not control all of the events that happen to you, but you can decide not to be reduced by them.

—Maya Angelou

Oh, wait. This COVID upheaval may be unique to our times, but upheaval is not unique to the human experience. Obviously I know we can't control life, but when all of the details felt especially out of control, it was good to remember that some circumstances are simply life on steroids and my responsibility is how I respond. Well, if that wasn't convicting, I'm not sure what was. I went from grumpy to grateful. I could see the truth in the words and how I needed to apply them immediately.

We walked around the corner in search of shade from the trees. I looked at my phone. Ninety-one degrees and it was only 10:40 a.m. The windows from the office wrapped around the building, and the next flower with yellow petals and a violet center felt like a big smile on a city street. In the center of the flower, written in black marker, were these words:

We must accept finite disappointment, but never give up infinite hope.

—Dr. Martin Luther King Jr.

Okay, boom. Finite disappointment was the mood of the day. Limitations felt never-ending. Everything in this life is finite with the exception of our souls and God. Those carry on past this temporal world. That infinite hope is what propels me forward. Way to sum up life there, Dr. King. If I want to live in the space of reality, I have no other choice than to accept what is finite. And to cling to the infinite hope found in Christ.

I know searching for infinite hope can sound like a simplistic Christian bumper sticker, but much of the Christian life is doing the same simple practices over and over. We don't just find hope once. We are in a constant pursuit of God's redemption because if we give up, we will be swallowed by the disappointment, heartache, and evil of the world. Our job is in the seeking. So how do we come back to infinite hope in the midst of our finite disappointments? We remember and think on the following:

The parameters of this world. We are bound by twenty-four hours in every day, seven days in every week, the seasons changing, and time moving on. We have no influence over the sun rising and setting. In some ways there is freedom in recognizing the places we have zero impact, because we can remember God controls those and we don't.

Our own limitations. When we remember that we are embodied souls and we are limited because we need sleep, nutrition, and exercise, we see our limitations in physical terms. We can only absorb so much information, fill so many needs, and complete a given number of tasks. There is freedom in recognizing our restrictions.

God's limitless nature. We go back to what is true about God. He is all-knowing, is without boundaries, and operates outside of time. There is not a finite amount of grace, patience, or goodness for him to offer the world. He is present in all places, goes before us, and remains behind when we are gone.

God's character. He is unchanging, so we can always know what to look for when searching for his evidence in the world. He is loving, merciful, and holy. He is just, creative, and gentle. When we find these characteristics reflected in people and places, we hear echoes of his presence.

QUESTIONS TO CONSIDER WHEN FACING FINITE DISAPPOINTMENT

» Will this disappointment have implications beyond today? This month? This year?

» Where does my disappointment stem from? What expectations were not met?

» Will there be ramifications from this disappointment that last into the next generation?

» How might God see an opportunity for his work in these circumstances?

» How could God's kingdom here on earth be strengthened from where I am today? How can this disappointment be redeemed for something good?

When we remember infinite hope, we are better able to see what is true and beautiful all around us. God's hope has not changed.

Pure Religion

Religion that God our Father accepts as pure and faultless is this: to look after orphans and widows in their distress and to keep oneself from being polluted by the world. (James 1:27)

Likely the most pivotal year of my life was when I was on staff and lived at the Dale House Project, a group home for teenagers aging out of the foster care system or finishing their parole sentence with the juvenile justice system in Colorado Springs. Just out of college, I lived on a neighborhood block with people only a few years younger than me in age but years ahead of me in heartache. The trauma they carried in their bodies and souls was crushing. And yet there we were, staff and residents alike, trying to live and love together. Trying to figure out where infinite hope was in the midst of what felt like infinite darkness.

What was pure in this place? Emotions. They were raw and real. As much as we all tried to cover up our feelings, they came out. For the kids, their pain of abandonment, betrayal, and mistreatment in the worst kinds of ways, usually by adults, was redirected as anger, grief, and a defensive posture. For the staff, our own childhood pain was echoed in our conversations and interactions with the kids, and we held it with a new understanding of how much deeper pain can go.

How did we see goodness here? In the darkness, the light is that much brighter. Hope was not a buzzword or something to be printed on a T-shirt. It was what we clung to on behalf of these teenagers. I was able to see how relevant the gospel was to hurting people. The deeper the well of pain, the more refreshing the living water that Jesus offered. The need for a redeemer was palpable, not just in their lives but suddenly in my own as well.

I was also able to see what serving Christ by looking after "the orphans" looked like on others. It was goodness personified. Was it neat, pretty, perfectly orchestrated? Of course not. Imperfect humans carrying out God's work never is. Was it sacrificial, tender, and true religion? In the best moments, yes.

Religion is a structure, a belief system, often a set of rules and norms that help organize and institutionalize ideas. It gets a bad name because by its very nature it can become impersonal and the rules can take over as they become systematized, even bureaucratic. James reminds us that religion, when carried out in the spirit of Christ—serving those who are forgotten—is the closest we can get to "pure." Christians often say their faith is not about rules but about a relationship with Jesus. I would never describe myself as a religious person because I'm not big on rituals or institutional structures. Rather, I'm big on Jesus's wellspring of mercy and tender love. Yet those from outside my faith would probably call me religious because I call myself a Christian and go to church on Sundays. My hope is that my actions match my words. That others see an authentic faith in an authentic life.

When we search for what is pure in this world, we are looking for those who care for the people in the shadows. Who is welcoming the stranger? The immigrant? The prisoner?

FINDING PURE RELIGION

» Make a list of vulnerable people in your immediate local community—those who are sick, hungry, tired, broke, and overwhelmed.

_____

_____

_____

_____

» Now make a list of people who are caring for them. Maybe these are organizations. Maybe they are individuals.

_____

_____

_____

_____

» Go through each list and pray for God's protection and provision for each person listed. Ask him to show you his goodness through the helpers' service and love.

Who is wiping the brow of the cancer patient? Taking the disabled neighbor's trash to the curb? Staying after school to meet with their struggling student's parents? When we look for religion in its pure form of caring for those who could get lost in the shuffle of life and society because they don't have the means, power, voice, or even words to speak up on their own behalf, we will find it in abundance.

A World of Low Expectations

It helps us to see God working through people. When living into pure religion, we are the best tangible reminder that God's goodness still permeates the world. The second part of James's description of pure religion is to "keep oneself from being polluted by the world." That's a charge that feels impossible to fulfill. But these steps we are taking through the guidance of Philippians 4:8—thinking on what is true, noble, right, and so on—are helping us to do just that. Seeking out goodness, mining through the pollution of toxic language and behavior around us, will in turn help us to live out religion that is "pure and faultless." The more we seek out evidence of God, the more we will find it, and the more it will change us. This will propel us to seek out that goodness even more. It is a cycle that fuels itself.

It's bad religion that has given Christianity a bad name. *Bad* religion would be the opposite of *pure* religion. It is not caring for the vulnerable. It is being "conformed to this world," to use a phrase we hear often in churchy circles referencing Romans 12:2: "Do not conform to the pattern of this world, but be transformed by the renewing of your mind. Then you will be able to test and approve what God's will is—his good, pleasing and perfect will." Or, as The Message says it,

> Don't become so well-adjusted to your culture that you fit into it without even thinking. Instead, fix your attention on God. You'll be changed from the inside out. Readily recognize what he wants from you, and quickly respond to it. Unlike the culture around you, always dragging you down to its level of immaturity, God brings the best out of you, develops well-formed maturity in you.

We have instruction not to just hop on the bandwagon of poor behavior that is often around us. Our attitudes in the workplace, at the grocery store, and on the PTA board should be different from the lowest common denominator. Others should know we won't be people who spout off in anger, who dip into the money, or who hold a grudge. We are called to a higher standard than the bar of low expectations.

Youth sports events, and more importantly parents at youth sports events, are a prime example of how we have lowered the bar for grown-up behavior. Go to any soccer field sideline and you can hear coaches and parents screaming at kids. I've been at basketball games where parents (and grandparents) have been involved in fights where police have been called. For kids' sports. I get the emotion of the moment. I understand how passion plays into cheering. My enthusiasm has sometimes surpassed what is called for. However, when we carry the stresses of our adult responsibilities onto the sidelines of a sports game and funnel our negative energy toward players, coaches, and referees, we are not demonstrating the holy work that is Christ within us. Self-control and gentleness, fruits of the Spirit, are not on display (to put it mildly).

Are we meant to be perfect people? Absolutely not. Are we supposed to remove ourselves or disengage from participating in what we know is poor behavior? Yes, I think that's clear. The more obvious behaviors are easy to call out. "Don't get in a fistfight at your daughter's basketball game" is a pretty easy one. It's the more subtle behaviors most of us need to watch for. Advocating for resources for our children that would take needed resources away from others' kids. Replying with sarcasm when someone needs a gentler response. Being more concerned about what we're wearing to church on Sunday than who we are inviting to join us there. We can justify many of our mixed motives—remember, none of us are "pure" on our own. When we seek out what is pure, we are recentering on what we are aiming for. The world gives us its set of standards, but God gives us another set.

Finding the Fruit

Years ago I led a local MOPS (Mothers of Preschoolers) group at my church. Every year we were given a theme by the larger ministry that helped guide conversations and topics for the meetings and made one year's programming feel different from another's. It also gave us a starting place for table decorations and all kinds of cute names for discussion groups, kids' classrooms, and newsletters. One year the theme was Fresh Fruit. As you can imagine, there was no lack of plastic fruit in bowls on the tables in our church basement meeting room. The theme was based on the fruit of the Spirit. As was intended, we as the leadership team spent a year studying what it meant to have the external fruit of internal growth.

As mothers of littles, we were a group desperate for more patience and gentleness. How about some self-control? With babies on our hips and diaper bags on our backs, we were running on empty and patience was running thin. Our mom guilt ran strong, and we knew all the ways we weren't experiencing joy or peace. Love was there—we were overwhelmed by how much we loved our children—but kindness was often determined by how well rested we were, and it wasn't the season of a good night's sleep.

As we sat around the church library table planning Christmas parties and determining substitute childcare policies, the group leaders talked about how we strive to muster up more gentleness but seem to always fall short. Though we couldn't will ourselves to produce the fruit on our own, you know what we became really good at? Seeing the fruit in each other. I could easily see faithfulness in these leaders, who dropped food off the night before a meeting even though they wouldn't be able to attend because of a sick child who needed to stay home. I saw kindness over and over again as women called each other to check in when someone shared something difficult the week before. I even saw patience as a leader led a small group discussion with a woman who always dominated the conversation. We gave each other the fuel we were desperate for by saying out loud, "You showed gentleness right there." That was the kind of refreshing talk that propelled us forward. Moms aren't often complimented for our behind-the-scenes work. We were calling out the good in each other.

Love, joy, peace, patience, kindness, goodness, faithfulness, gentleness, and self-control (Gal. 5:22–23). When the Holy Spirit is stirring in us, shaping our thought patterns, we can't help but have these fruit blossoms appear and grow into more substantial fruit. A lemon tree doesn't decide to grow lemons; it was created to do so, and under the right conditions it produces lots of good and flavorful fruit. A lemon tree doesn't give us hamburgers or broccoli; it gives us lemons. The Holy Spirit doesn't produce jealousy, bitterness, or selfishness. The Spirit produces love, joy, and peace. When we're looking for hope in the world, for God's goodness, there is no purer expression than these traits that result from God working in us. And when we see these traits in others, it is a gift to name them, because sometimes we

SPOTTING FRUIT

» Consider love, joy, peace, patience, kindness, goodness, faithfulness, gentleness, and self-control.
» Think of someone you know who displays one or more of these qualities in their daily life. Send them a text or write them a note, letting them know the good you see growing in and through them.
» Choose one trait to ask the Holy Spirit to grow in you. Pray for God to give you opportunities to grow and produce that fruit.

need someone else to remind us that we are producing fruit even when the conditions are harsh.

Just like with truth, sometimes it is easier to see what is not pure in order to know what is. Have you ever had a conversation with someone and left feeling a little bit icky, but you weren't sure why? Have you thought technically something is accurate, but it isn't right? Or is there a person you've never quite trusted because you don't feel like you are getting their true selves?

> Here are six things GOD hates,
>> and one more that he loathes with a passion:
>>> eyes that are arrogant,
>>> a tongue that lies,
>>> hands that murder the innocent,
>>> a heart that hatches evil plots,
>>> feet that race down a wicked track,
>>> a mouth that lies under oath,
>>> a troublemaker in the family.
>> (Prov. 6:16–19 MSG)

Often it is easier for us to detect what God hates, or what is impure, than what is pure. Just as the darkness helps us to more easily see the light, the things that are not of God can help us detect the things that are. When we see what is impure, we can then ask, *What is the opposite of this?* That is where we'll see God's goodness.

When you see a bully, where are the people who are standing up to that person? That is goodness.

When you see a faulty system, where are the ones who are calling for improvement? That is goodness.

When you see someone trying to ruin an honest person's reputation, where are those who are honoring that person? That is goodness.

There is something in our spirits that is repelled by sin, by turning our backs on God. So when we feel that inner tension or nudge, we can pause, examine it, and ask ourselves, *Why is this making me uncomfortable? Is it because this is what God hates?* If so, the next question is, *Where is God's counteraction of goodness? Where do I see the opposite playing out in a person, system, or place?*

Pure Perspectives

I had just experienced a big transition in my work life. It required stepping away from something I'd felt called to for many years. I could not look at my own life with clear eyes. Every angle of the decision impacted something I cared about: my time and energy for my family, my stress level, my income, and my career trajectory and potential opportunities.

Our perspectives on most things are clouded. They are colored by our life experiences, hurts, wins, and information. Sometimes when we look for God's goodness in the world, the lenses we see through distort what is real and pure. Sometimes we can admit that we are unable to see with clarity, but many times we cannot, and our blind spots prevent us from recognizing the goodness in front of us. As I transitioned out of my job, I needed the wisdom of fellow Christ followers who had no personal investment in the outcomes of my decisions and who would not be impacted in any way and therefore could offer some unique, objective insights as outsiders looking in on where God was working. I needed a mastermind group. My friend Krista and I decided to start one because of our own need for this outside, Christ-centered perspective, but we immediately found that others were craving it too.

God's viewpoint is clear. His vista is not muddled by weather, distorted by time, or limited by how the world is playing out before us. We will never hold God's perspective, but the closer we can get to it within our human limitations, the purer our vantage point with which to see the world will be and the more easily and accurately we'll be able to identify goodness. Getting closer to God's viewpoint is wrapped up in being closer to him. Our knowledge of, and more importantly our relationship with, him helps sweep the fog away and offers clarity. But how do we get closer to God's viewpoint?

> *Read Scripture with new eyes.* As people of faith, we've
> likely read some stories in our Bibles dozens of
> times. The familiarity of the words can feel comfort-
> ing, but it can also sound bland and rote. We can
> almost become numb as we reread the text. Ap-
> proaching the story from a different viewpoint can
> give us new insights to who God is, and that will in
> turn help us to find his goodness in the world.
>
> Questions to ask when wanting a fresh
> perspective:
>
>> *How does the story change when seen from a particular*
>> *character's viewpoint? What does that insight indi-*
>> *cate about God's character?*

*How would Jesus retell the story? What examples would
he use today to make that same point?*

*How would my "neighbor" read this story—my neighbor
from across the street and from across the world?*

*What details would be important to my neighbors? What
do those details indicate about God?*

Cut out the junk food. Just as we want to fill our minds
and hearts with who God is, we want to cut out that
which is not helping us love God or our neighbors
better. When wanting to be healthy, we not only
increase nutritious foods but we also cut out junk
food. Gossip, sarcasm, sensational "news," and por-
nography are all things we can consume that do not
help us hear God's voice.

Questions to ask when determining if you are
consuming "junk food":

*Am I better able to love God because of what I'm con-
suming? Am I better able to love my neighbors?*

*Does this give me helpful information or a helpful per-
spective about God and about my neighbors so that I
can better love both?*

*Could I be using my time in another way that better
prepares me or enables me to love God and love my
neighbors?*

Increase the margins. In a world where "busy" is equated
with "important," we can run around in a crazed, ex-
hausted state, attempting to fit enough responsibilities for four people into one life. God created us to

have rhythms of rest every year, every week, and every day. When we slow down, we are usually better able to hear and see God because we have enough time to listen and watch for where he might be evident.

Questions to ask when determining the margins in your life:

> *Do I have time daily to listen for God's voice? To watch for his goodness?*
>
> *Do I have time built into my weekly schedule for rest?*
>
> *If so, when are those times? Where are those places?*
>
> *If not, where can I intentionally build in time to be watchful for the holy at work?*

Ask the Holy Spirit for help. We have access to a holy and pure perspective when the Holy Spirit brings forward new insights, questions, thoughts, or pictures. The more we commune in prayer with the Spirit, the more we will be able to recognize the Spirit's movement. Like any relationship, this takes time, patience, and listening.

Questions to ask when wanting to access the Holy Spirit:

> *Do I believe I have access to the Holy Spirit?*
>
> *Have I heard the Spirit's voice or felt the Spirit's nudge before?*
>
> *If so, how did that feel?*
>
> *If not, am I willing to keep trying as I search for God's goodness in this life?*

Recognize we have limitations. Yes, we can pursue God's pure perspective, but we will always be limited. We may sense God's peace or direction over a decision, but we will never have true understanding. This takes the pressure off to always have the "right" answer. We don't know what we're doing as we stumble through this life, so let's live in the freedom of the unknown.

Questions to ask when considering your limitations:

> *What do I hope to know of God? From God? Is that realistic?*
>
> *How can I use my five senses to experience God?*
>
> *How can I see him in people and places?*
>
> *How can I show God gratitude for the ways he does reveal himself to me?*

PRUNING FOR FRUIT

Instead of determining to add more to your life to gain God's perspective, name what you can cut out. Tree branches are pruned to encourage growth and fruit. There is a good chance you need less of one thing rather than more of something else. What can you cut from your "junk food" consumption, schedule, or expectations that will open you up to more of the Holy Spirit?

How can I work toward experiencing his goodness given my human limitations?

Love Your Enemies

There is nothing purer than the good fruit of the Spirit working in us to extend love to those who have wronged us. The idea of having an "enemy" sounds juvenile. However, there are people in the world who make me feel defensive, who get me riled up, or who have legitimately wronged me. Now that I've recognized the world is not full of my BFFs, shouldn't I just try to avoid those who make me upset? But wait, isn't this how we end up in our self-created echo chambers and tribes in the first place? Where we say we value diversity, but we don't want the discomfort it brings when it means being with people who live differently, think differently, and believe differently than we do? How can we see God's goodness in the world if we're only willing to be in spheres where his goodness is reflected back to us in ways that feel palpable and pleasant?

In Matthew 5:43–48, Jesus says,

You're familiar with the old written law, "Love your friend," and its unwritten companion, "Hate your enemy." I'm challenging that. I'm telling you to love your enemies. Let them bring out the best in you, not the worst. When someone gives you a hard time, respond with the supple moves of prayer, for then you are working out of your true selves, your God-created selves. This is what God does. He gives his best—the sun to warm and the rain to nourish—to everyone, regardless: the good and bad, the nice and nasty.

If all you do is love the lovable, do you expect a bonus? Anybody can do that. If you simply say hello to those who greet you, do you expect a medal? Any run-of-the-mill sinner does that.

In a word, what I'm saying is, *Grow up.* You're kingdom subjects. Now live like it. Live out your God-created identity. Live generously and graciously toward others, the way God lives toward you. (MSG)

If this isn't convicting, I'm not sure what is. Jesus is telling us to grow up. Live like the kingdom subjects we are. "When someone gives you a hard time, respond with the supple moves of prayer, for then you are working out of your true selves, your God-created selves." This is the key to loving our enemies. When God is working in us, we are more likely to be able to step through the hurt and pain and work toward giving them our best. That fruit of the Spirit, the gentleness and self-control we try to muster up on our own, is more likely to grow if we are allowing the Holy Spirit to marinate our hearts and produce this fruit. Then when he does, it

PRAY FOR YOUR ENEMIES

Pray for someone who has wronged you. Ask God to grow the fruit of the Spirit in you so that you can respond in a true and beautiful way.

surprises the world (and sometimes even us) because it is so counterintuitive and countercultural.

So when that one neighbor who always lets their dog poop on my lawn or that one parent on the football team who always yells with more intensity than I prefer is doing their unintentional—or even intentional—best to get on my last nerve, the proper first response is prayer? I state this as a question because, for the record, my first response is not prayer. But Jesus reminds me of what pure love looks like. It is displaying the fruit of his Spirit in a way that extends mercy and grace. That is pure love for a hurting world.

God Has Not Left Us: Forgiveness

It was on Good Friday that a friend from college posted a question on Facebook about forgiveness. She was drawing from the headlines of the day, but the themes of her post were familiar. Essentially, she asked, "How can one group of Christians so easily forgive and another be so quick to judge?" I get it. I feel this "What gives?" question all the time too. Why do some lean into forgiveness when they are justifiably hurt and wronged, and why do others seem to be entertained by pointing out the missteps of those around them?

I don't often engage in big questions on Facebook, but if someone is asking a question and I think I am uniquely positioned to offer some insight, I do. My answer went something like this:

> I don't know why some Christians forgive the big offenses easily and others hold on tightly to the small stuff. I do know that forgiveness is the premise of our faith. For God so loved

the world he came. Today on Good Friday we remember God's commitment to forgiveness. The more we recognize our own need for forgiveness, the more willing we are to extend forgiveness to others.

God's grace, his unmerited gift of forgiveness, is the driver of our faith. It is proof of his pure love for us. So why, as my friend asked, don't we lead with it? Because we have been hurt. Because that sinful nature we carry around in our DNA has pride as the filter for our interactions with others, pushing us toward blame and blinding us to our own need for forgiveness. Because we believe we must *feel* forgiveness before we offer it. Because we think forgiving someone relieves them of responsibility to make amends. These are all barriers that keep us from doing what is right and extending forgiveness. Obviously the nature of the offense and the depth of pain it causes determine the difficulty. Yet when we extend it, we are able to demonstrate our purest reflection of God's goodness to our neighbors.

The fruit is good. The fruit leads to forgiveness. When we seek out both, we can't help but see there is goodness still to be found. If looking for Jesus and his hope are the key to finding what is pure, there is no better evidence than forgiveness.

A Prayer for
WHATEVER IS PURE

Lord, we ask that you remove the things you hate from our hearts:

> "eyes that are arrogant,
> a tongue that lies,
> hands that murder the innocent,
> a heart that hatches evil plots,
> feet that race down a wicked track,
> a mouth that lies under oath,
> a troublemaker in the family." (Prov. 6:16–19 MSG)

As we wipe these away, help us to see what remains.
Give us . . .

eyes that cry tears of empathy,

tongues that speak what is true and good,

hands that comfort ailing bodies,

hearts that celebrate the victories of others,

feet that run the road of generosity,

mouths that speak promises kept,

leaders who unify with integrity.

We know that when we extract what is not of you, we are left with faith, hope, and love.

And the greatest of these is your essence: pure and lasting love.

May we be Jesus people known for making faith, hope, and love popular because we can't quit the creative ways they appear in our daily activities.

May our actions make seen what is unseen of you and enhance your reputation.

May we recognize your goodness in babies' eyelashes, ocean currents, and second chances.

Holy Spirit, whisper through our spirits and thoughts to keep your well of goodness in the foreground of our vision.

When we see the world through your microscope, we will see your goodness manifested.

Amen.

QUESTIONS *for* REFLECTION

1. How might you approach finite disappointments in light of infinite hope?

2. Where do you see pure religion played out? What attributes of God do you see in the people who are caring for the could-be forgotten?

3. How have you allowed yourself to be shaped by the culture of low expectations? How does that hinder you from seeing God's goodness in the world?

4. When has the fruit of the Spirit surprised you? When has God given you more love, joy, peace, patience, kindness, goodness, faithfulness, gentleness, or self-control than you expected?

5. Who might you need to forgive? Are you able to move toward forgiveness even if your heart isn't feeling it?

Faith in God's Goodness

As a nurse married to a physician, Heather knew she was sick. The symptoms were acute enough that she went to her doctor and then to the emergency room in the middle of a pandemic shutdown. Though she was bracing herself for anything (she'd had her fair share of difficult conversations with patients throughout her career), her stage 4 stomach cancer diagnosis still came as a shock. Heather and her husband, Bob, knew this was a cancer that was often vicious because patients don't show symptoms until it has spread.

Heather was suddenly faced with grieving her life plans. Would watching her grandkids grow up, her work as a nurse at a high school for pregnant and parenting teens, and her daily rhythms with Bob be coming to a close? Was she facing the end of her life?

Heather remembered a woman she had known years earlier when she and Bob worked at a clinic for the homeless in Washington, DC. Heather admired how this friend, who was given a terminal diagnosis, didn't fight the reality of her situation but embraced it. "Instead of saying 'Why me?'" Heather said, "she had more of an attitude of 'Why not me?' That stuck with me, and I decided I wanted to be like her." It's Heather's natural bent to be grateful for the good things in her life—her marriage, her children's marriages, her health up to this point. She and Bob have lived and served in Africa; Washington, DC; Chicago; and most recently Denver. When reflecting on her life, Heather thinks of all her experiences and mostly of the people she has had the chance to know; they come to the forefront of her mind.

Right after her diagnosis, Heather's friends Pam and Mark said they wanted to organize a virtual prayer gathering to pray for her regularly while she was going through chemo. One of the benefits of pandemic life was that people were growing more accustomed to using this type of group technology for purposes as intimate as prayer. Heather was overwhelmed with the number of people who participated, representing all the places they'd lived, including her childhood Sunday school friends from New Jersey and cousins who now lived overseas. She reconnected with friends she hadn't talked to in years. It was humbling to have so many from around the world gather virtually every few weeks because of her and pray on her behalf. She described it as "a taste of heaven."

Chemo has done its work on Heather, and she is feeling better physically, though she knows that with a stage 4 diagnosis, the cancer won't be disappearing. This is a game of holding off, not curing. As the disease has slowed and her energy is up a bit, Heather can face each day to live with new plans: a trip to the zoo with her daughter and grandchildren, a phone call with a friend far away, lunch with her husband, who quit his job because of daily COVID exposure and her intensely compromised immune system. Some naps and doctor appointments are fit in there too, but Heather is actively seeking the good in the midst of the hard. She is reconnecting with people because without work and while quarantining at home, she has more time.

"I was really sick. I felt terrible and had lots of complications," Heather remembers. "God was there. He helped me." She says heaven, whatever that looks like, feels more real and closer than it ever has.

The unexpected could have derailed Heather. She has her moments of sadness, but she can't shake her gratitude. Yet she doesn't have an answer to the question "Why me?" or, as she prefers, "Why not me?"

"I don't know why God would allow this," she says. "I know he promises good things for us and he promises to be with us. I know God will be with me through it."

Part 5

WHERE DID ALL
the GLITTER GO?

Whatever is lovely . . .

PHILIPPIANS 4:8

*Blessed are they who see beautiful things in humble
places where other people see nothing.*

CAMILLE PISSARRO

W"here did all of the glitter go?"
My two youngest girls were sitting at the bar
facing our kitchen, playing with slime, the Play-
Doh of older kids. Pounding it, rolling it, and squeezing the
soft goop with their hands. I don't understand the obses-
sion, but there was something calming in the tactile knead-
ing happening. The prepackaged slime came with specks

155

of glitter, and as the girls worked the slime through their fingers, pieces of it were coming off on their hands, but there was no glitter. It was disappearing. And so Gracelynn wondered where it was going.

It struck me that lately much of my life had lost its glitter. Or at least I was having a hard time finding it. The carefree nature of days, the laughter, and even the excitement of waking up in the morning seemed gone! When each of my girls was a toddler, still sleeping in a crib, I could hear her voice through the baby monitor in the morning. I would go into her room and find her standing, holding the rails with an anticipation that I was going to walk through that door and we were about to have the most excellent day ever! Where are the days when anyone is thrilled to see me when I walk into a room? How do we welcome the morning with the joy and excitement that God is making the sun rise again? We have lost our sense of wonder at the miracles evident in each moment. Every breath is something to be cheered, but I for one could work on my cheering.

The Message paraphrases *lovely* in Philippians 4:8 as "compelling." That makes sense. We are drawn to the lovely, to beauty. Art has a long history with the Christian church because beautiful things elicit an instinctive response of awe in us. For centuries the church has supported artists to make music and paint. God makes beautiful things, so when we see his creation or beauty in what others have made, we remember that his goodness permeates the world. From the majestic Rocky Mountains to the colors of tropical paradise, we find the compelling in the natural world. We also see how our created environments can establish a sense of peace and calm (or not!). And, of course, we find God's lovely goodness reflected in humanity. From the mother mesmerized by her newborn to those newly in love, we have phases in our lives when other people captivate us. This is because people reflect God's image. Living in an embodied world, we can search out and appreciate the tangible creation and call it good—or beautiful, as a further reflection of God's goodness.

If truth, honor, and justice are the meat of our goodness meal, the lovely is the dessert. It's also the table setting, the music, the wine served. It's the flair that turns a house into a home, a meeting into a party, and a series of days into a life well lived. It's what compels us toward a space or a person. It is seeing the holy revealed in the details of life, often without us knowing that is what's drawing us in.

In the Beginning

Derek and I found the first days in the hospital with a newborn sacred. With each girl handed to us, swaddled and miniature (except for the third, who at eight and a half pounds felt not so mini), we were ambushed with the miracle of what we call life. Two of my deliveries happened in the afternoon, and two of my labors were in the dark hours of early morning. It did not matter when each girl arrived; she had tiny, fairy-sized fingernails and nostrils, and we felt an overwhelming sense of awe. Though there were moments when I could barely keep my eyes open, I was overwhelmed with gratitude that God had made life and we were able to witness it up close in a way that made us love and appreciate him more.

157

Once we were home, the reality of responsibilities and, after the first child, the other already mobile and verbal children demanded our attention in the way that people who speak in bullhorn-level volumes do. The stresses of life and continued exhaustion from sleep-wrecked days with a newborn quickly distracted us from sitting in the miracle for too long. That's why those hospital days sit so fondly in our memories. They were dedicated to accepting the gifts God was offering in miracles compounded that make a new person. How many things had to go right for each girl to come into creation? How much goodness was harnessed and manifested to culminate in her arrival? If we wanted to see God's goodness, we could find it in each gift of a child. And we could feel it acutely right from the start.

From the very beginning of the world as we understand it, God made beautiful things. He formed light, clay, ocean tides, and root systems. He made antlers, whiskers, and claws for hunting. He formed deserts, mountain ranges, and seasons that change with equal parts predictability and wonder. It is no surprise we describe a view as breathtaking. His glorious creation has the ability to stop us and take our breath away. When we see a snow-capped mountain range, a star-swept sky, or a sunset of pink and orange, we can't help but get a hint of the vast power and beauty of the God who formed it.

Creation

Creation can capture our attention in such a way that we pause, look up, and consider for just a second how the lovely was made and why. It brings to mind and spirit a sense that we are part of something much bigger than our own little plot of space on this earth. God's majesty is found in the forest with trees so tall they block out the sunlight, in the mountain river as it rushes past, and at the ocean's edge as we feel the power and hear the roar of the waves crashing on the sand. His goodness is reflected in the details. The way our ecosystems are balanced and work together, how water evaporates, and how microbes do whatever it is that microbes do. God attended to the big and the small in his making of the beautiful.

God called all of his creation good.

But in my life I'm seldom standing at the ocean's edge, I often can't see the western sky because of my neighbor's roofline, and I'm looking ahead or down at a screen rather than up, and the natural world goes unnoticed. I lose the wonder because I get caught up in the busyness and don't take time to notice. God's creation is always just an open door away from me, even though I live in a busy city neighborhood where the view from our living room is a street where cars, people, and dogs go by at rapid speed. No vistas to behold. No breathtaking mountain ranges. And yet there is fresh(ish) air, birds to listen for, and sunshine to sit in.

It's no surprise that being outside impacts people's mental health. Tethered to our screens, we can experience climate-controlled lives that easily forget the wild, wonderful world that our Creator made. The crisp air on our face, or better yet, the rain or snow, snaps us back into our place in the universe, and we remember God is bigger than the latest news feed. The earth is still spinning, and the pundits of the day cannot control the trees growing or the flowers budding. I'll admit I like climate control. I enjoy heat in the winter and a little cool air in the summer. And yet I know that even in my city life, stepping outside brings another perspective—one of a bigger world and truly of hope—that helps me.

I have one girl in particular who loves camping. I suspect it's because she loves the undistracted time her parents and sisters offer her. With no chores to do (other than those endless camping ones, of course) and lots of treats packed, she can think of nothing better than being in the elements with the people she loves. The rest of us weigh the benefits of sitting around a campfire against the poor sleep we get and the work at home before and after, but Giulianna thinks life should be one big camping trip. As the mom, I can think of nothing more exhausting. But we don't have to make our creation excursions backpacking trips or sailing vacations that require days away. We can focus on the small doses, the reminder that in all seasons God is at work. We do that by stepping outside.

Play, dining, and exercise are three activities we do on a daily basis (well, exercise if we're disciplined). Incorporating some outside time in one of those three areas every day can help us remember what is true and beautiful about God our Creator.

Play. I recognize outside play for kids may require a different level of supervision or involvement for parents than the inside version. Whether we take a book to the backyard while littles play in the baby pool or walk to the playground down the street, the good news is our children playing outside can help us be outside too. But maybe we're the ones playing.

Maybe it's painting on the patio or talking on the phone to your cousin on your front steps. Doing something you love, and doing it outside, helps you see the lovely.

Dining. Coffee on the patio, snacks on a blanket in the park, dinner with candles on a warm evening. There is something about eating al fresco that helps us celebrate what is lovely. Perhaps because we are forced to sit during a meal, it creates enough of a pause in our frantic schedules to notice what is happening around and above us. Perhaps it's being together, if we're eating with others, that helps us see the lovely more clearly. Or maybe it's just the combination of God's provision in food and sky that reminds us that life still has some good.

Exercise. My workout routine usually involves pushing Play on Demand. I continue the screen life inside, even when I'm moving my body. We have treadmills and gyms and workout rooms where we exercise and multitask. Instead, decide to go for a walk or run outside. Invite a friend to join you. Move your muscles, breathe in through your nose, and feel the elements on your skin. Experience the day that the Lord has made, and thank him for your body (aches and limitations and all) in the midst of his beautiful world.

On a warm November day, we drove over to my mom's house and had a COVID-friendly picnic in her backyard. We'd never had a November outdoor lunch, but because we

GET OUTSIDE

Go outside for five minutes. Set an alarm and close your eyes. Listen. What do you hear? Smell? Feel on your skin? What does this tell you? Slow your breathing and experience creation, however quiet or noisy it is. After five minutes, open your eyes and see if you notice anything different. Colors? Structures? Plants? Animals? People?

could in a time when we were limiting indoor activities, we did. She would say her incredible garden wasn't at its prime, but the late fall landscape offered a different perspective. Though we were bundled in sweatshirts and coats, we could feel the sun on our backs and consider that we were grateful for the moment. For the day. That God had gifted us with good food, good company, and good weather. Had we done nothing (which was our other option given the pandemic life), we would have missed out on noticing all the goodness around us. Noticing is what we are practicing.

Using Our Senses

When we go to a friend's house for dinner and smell the food cooking in the kitchen two rooms over, hear the music playing a gentle melody, and see the dim light of a fire or candles flickering in the living room, we feel both expected and expectant. We are expected in that someone prepared for our arrival. The details of their home tell us before a word is spoken that our hosts knew we were coming and did some work to prepare. Because we know they cared for us enough to do that, we are expectant that something, hopefully good, is going to happen while we are there. This type of environment involves both creating and reflecting. Whenever we create goodness through the details of our environment, we are reflecting God's goodness.

Our senses can be a road map for experiencing what is lovely. Surely we can experience horror, stench, and death through them as well, but if we see what we are looking for, the same idea can be applied to taste, smell, sound, and touch. I think of the baby just born and how skin-to-skin contact, laying the newborn on the mother's bare chest directly after birth, is distinctly bonding. UNICEF says both mothers and babies respond physically and emotionally when they experience this significant touch after delivery. Babies will relax, tend to search for the mother's breast, and have their heart rate and temperature regulated.[1] A newborn can recognize their mother's or father's voice, quieting down when these familiar people are speaking. Some studies show that newborns are drawn to their mother's smell, especially the smell of her breast milk.[2] All of this points to God's design for our senses to help us navigate through the world. He has created us to use our senses for bonding from birth.

Our senses can give us a taste of God's goodness as well. This often requires slowing down, paying attention to our environments, and making a conscious note of what we taste, hear, see, smell, and feel. Mindfulness practices can help us with this, making us more aware of our current surroundings and giving us a break from the constant distractions of our screens and schedules. Once we are more aware of our surroundings, we can ask how they point to God's existence.

Our senses can also point us toward God's creativity. Flavors and smells, colors and sonatas, and the texture of hard wood, granite, or fur can help us see his creative mark. When we see him at work, we can more easily bond with him too. Psalm 34:8 says, "Taste and see that the LORD is good." He has given us wonderful things to experience and made our bodies to absorb them. He created us, in part, to experience the rest of creation.

Taste. Slow down when eating. Try foods from other countries and cultures. Eat produce when it's in season. Choose whole foods that aren't processed. Eat for health and for pleasure. Avoid having a limitation (calorie-count) mindset when eating. Food is meant to be enjoyed.

Sound. Listen to the leaves blowing in the wind. Play instrumental music as you get ready for the day. Also introduce silence into your routine so you don't get addicted to background noise. Sit quietly and listen for God's voice. We can hear his goodness if we listen.

Sight. Look at the unique features of your father's nose. Study the details of a leaf or a piece of grass. Observe how your children run in the front yard. We can learn a lot about the world through our vision, and we can appreciate God's goodness when we watch how his creation is operating in the world.

Smell. Close your eyes briefly as you go on a walk, stand in front of the stove, or hug someone in your family and notice the smell. The only sense fully developed in the womb, smell is closely linked to our childhood memories because smell and emotion are stored as a single memory.[3] Consider how given smells were impacted by your life experiences.

Touch. Give someone a shoulder squeeze. Add soft throw blankets to your seating areas. Jump into a swimming pool. Walk barefoot in your garden. Pet your pup. God gives us the sensation of touch, and it helps inform us of the world. From a mother feeling a baby's first kicks in the womb to a high five at a basketball game, we know our bodies can be used to communicate and experience God's goodness.

FOCUSING ON YOUR SENSES

Choose one of your five senses. Notice for a day how you use it. Notice how it informs you of the world and how it shows you God's goodness. Offer God a prayer of thanksgiving every time you use that sense.

God designed our bodies to interact with the world. Our fight-or-flight instinct serves to protect us from danger. Our senses can also alert us to God's glory. If we pay attention to them, we will be better at noticing the good all around us.

The Practice of Noticing

From my dining room I could see an unusual purple tone to the sky, with the more typical pink and orange sunset clouds peeking over my neighbor's roofline. It was screaming color, and being inside wasn't helping me hear. I grabbed my purse and car keys and left the house a few minutes earlier than needed to pick Gracelynn up from soccer practice. The sky needed to be admired, and sitting in my car parked next to the soccer field would be a great place to do the admiring. Depending on the wait at the stoplight, our house is only four minutes from the park. By the time I turned the corner toward my typical parking spot, the sky had already mellowed, the colors dimmed, the vibrancy gone.

My first thought was, *What if I hadn't looked up earlier? I would have totally missed it.* I could have been mad at myself for not leaving the house sooner, disappointed I didn't capture what I did see with a click of my phone, or just sad my vision for five minutes of quiet and sunset at dusk wasn't playing out as I'd thought. Those are all responses I've had before. This time, though, I felt gratitude for having seen a roofline-obstructed view of the most vibrant moments of the evening's sunset. I'm not sure where that focus on gratitude came from, but I sat in it for a second.

The beautiful often comes when we don't expect it and leaves with as little fanfare. Its presence is the same whether we notice it or not. In our search for goodness, it is to our benefit to stop and pay attention

This entire book is about noticing the details in unexpected places. Often that involves a practice of allowing ourselves to be surprised, to have expectations not met but in the best way possible. It takes our minds and expectations a bit to catch up as the beauty unfolds around us, but once they do, we see how God has done a work we didn't even know to ask for. We can find the lovely through delightful surprises.

I've often had to wait and work on noticing God's goodness. These unexpected events have included

- a pregnancy
- a rejected book proposal
- a stop at a garage sale
- a disappointing college financial-aid package
- a snow day off of school
- a rained-out soccer tournament

Though all of these events were initially surprises, many of them unwelcome, in the end they all produced good results. Actually, better results than I knew to ask for. Some of the noticing of God's goodness took time, but with time came perspective. A stop at a garage sale to look at a lawn mower turned into placing an offer on the house we now live in. A rained-out soccer tournament that we traveled states away to get to became a memorable trip with other families and hours of conversation with friends as we sat in hotel rooms and listened to the thunder outside. With every unexpected turn, I try to pause long enough to ask myself, *God, is there good here that I didn't even know to ask for?* This pause is the discipline that leads to noticing so I can see the compelling evidence of God at work. Those unexpected events helped me notice

- our family who has room for one more
- the deepening friendship over the shared fiasco of a trip
- the excuse to stay in jammies all day and watch movies and make cookies

When put this way, it all sounds magical. But I had to look through some difficult realities to notice the good. Work deadlines still needed to be met even though my kids had the day off from school. A career path that was ramping up and the cost of childcare, not to mention the energy of having another child, would likely put some of my plans aside. The dream college that would have looked quite impressive on my résumé would have left me starting my adult life in debt. There was disappointment to peer through to find what was compelling.

Compelling

In design, there are elements that make a space "work," from color and pattern combinations to physical spacing and blocking. I can walk into a room and feel more or less relaxed as a result of the physical space. Classrooms and offices are designed with tasks or creativity in mind. As we set up our home for pandemic virtual school, we learned about "hard spaces" and "soft spaces." Hard spaces are desks and chairs intended for computing math equations and practicing spelling words. Soft spaces are places to curl up with a book and enjoy the words and adventures in a setting that encourages imagination. Both are compelling for different reasons. One makes you want to get to work; another lets your mind wander.

I know that I'm drawn to both the hard and the soft spaces of life. Sometimes I want to get the task done, and other times I'm ready to snuggle in. If pressed, I could probably say why I'm compelled by something, but often it's more subconscious. I'm not sure why I like a room, I just do. Another person may walk into a room and begin to rattle off all the reasons it has a good "feel" to it. The faux fur rug, fabric pillows, and beanbag chair give off an essence of "cozy."

Two things are true here. First, we often don't know why we're compelled by something. Second, someone else is often intentional in making the lovely happen.

As with rooms, we are usually compelled by something and someone because of how they make us feel. Like a space, a person can be welcoming and warm. An idea or theory can be intriguing because it validates a part of us. We are compelled by something because we like what it says about who we are and who God is. Again, for me this is often not a conscious thought process. Rather, I have to stop and consider why something draws me in. *What about it appeals to me?* This very question will not only help me understand myself better; it will also help me intentionally seek out what I find compelling or lovely. I can then in turn be more intentional about incorporating those compelling attributes into my practices for others' sake.

I know my friend Erin is someone I can relax around, so I ask myself, *What about her makes me want to be with her?* I find her to be safe—she allows me to be who I am without judgment. If I feel more confident in tackling my daily stresses after talking to Erin, it's because she listens without distraction, and she says back to me what she's heard so she and I both know she understood. I can celebrate that trait in her, call it out, and thank her for it. I can also look for it in other people. It's something I value, and therefore if I see it in others, I'm celebrating the lovely in them. But then I can also be more intentional in reflecting that attribute to others.

I believe if we are healthy people, other healthy people and patterns compel us. But if we are living in unhealth, we can get sucked into patterns that draw us in and are anything but lovely. This in some ways brings us back to truth. If we are operating from lies about who we are (we're unworthy, undeserving, even uninteresting), we can be drawn to relationships with people, food, sex, or substances that reflect those lies. But if we are operating out of truth (we are created, separated, forgiven, redeemed), we are confident that our value has already been determined and we are compelled by patterns that reflect our holy identity back to us. This doesn't mean we surround ourselves with people who offer only flattery, or organize our lives in such a way that we're never uncomfortable. It means we root ourselves in the truth of who God is and who he says we are, and then we will be quicker to recognize his character and pattern in others. God's goodness feeds on itself. The more we know of him, the more the things that reflect his goodness compel us, and the more easily we'll see those things when we seek them.

AN EXERCISE FOR THE COMPELLED

» Consider a space you like.
» How do you feel when you are there?
» How do others feel when they are there?
» What is it about that space that makes you want to be there?
» Are there ways you can make a space compelling for someone else?

We Are Makers

We humans are the only creatures made in God's image (Gen. 1:27). Therefore, like him, we are makers, creators, and feelers. Let's not forget that God is a maker of good things. "God saw all that he had made, and it was very good" (Gen. 1:31). We are a good creation, and we are attracted to what is good. The most powerful ways we find what is good and lovely are in what God has made: his world and his people.

Because we are people made in God's image, we are makers. As we reflect his nature in the creative process, we are reflecting his goodness. It's a cycle that keeps feeding and regenerating itself. We reflect God, so we make. What we make further reflects God. We recognize his compelling nature reflected in creation, which then draws us back to him. That is why art can be so powerful. It is a reflection of our God-made world using God-given brains, hands, feelings, and thoughts to evoke a reaction from other image bearers. The Christian church has almost always been a patron of the arts. I assume this is why. Art can bring us closer to the true and beautiful and the holy experience of living on earth.

We experience our artistic tendencies in different expressions. Music, writing, and visual arts are all ways that we formally worship God. But so is architecture, as we consider how cathedrals and chapels have been designed for centuries, or fashion, as we understand how clothing expresses our experiences. When we make something out of nothing in physical space, whether it's a building or a choir robe, we are making statements, direct and indirect, about God's goodness. Of course, just as in all things good, the creation doesn't need to be an overt representation of God for it to be breathtaking. We see his goodness in all the ways our fellow people are makers when they reflect the gospel story of creation, separation, reconciliation, and redemption. Not all things made are good on their own; I'd argue that some forms of art are exploitive and damaging. But if they point toward the larger narrative, even if they cause us discomfort, they serve a purpose that makes us stop and gaze and consider the eternal.

We can appreciate what is lovely in what others make, and we can participate in God's invitation to cocreate with him. We can plant a garden, tell a bedtime story, and sing with the music on our Spotify playlist. We can make a video, grill a burger, or hang twinkle lights in a bedroom. We often think of the "making" process as something that must be monumental and elaborate, when we are actually making all day long. Many of our making tasks, like making beds, feel mundane or at least unnoteworthy. Baking a blueberry coffee cake is not equivalent to painting the *Mona Lisa*, after all. But it's not supposed to be.

Our days are not filled with masterpieces that are meant to memorialize us forever. They are filled with opportunities to add a little bit of beauty to the world—in the small details of life that move a room to a sanctuary, words to an idea, a recipe to a meal. And soon that little bit of beauty builds on itself and becomes something bigger. I write books one sentence at a time. My mom tends her garden one plant at a time. My husband laid hardwood floors in our living room one plank at a time. We are to enjoy what is lovely, call it out, and then reflect it back to the world. One cup of sugar, one paint stroke, one pulled weed at a time.

Ways We Are Makers

I can hear the inner dialogue now. *But some people are truly creative. Their contribution to the world is more significant. Their creations are just plain lovely.* The "Pinterest fail" makes fun of our attempt to re-create perfection standards when we fall incredibly short. I've laughed at my own attempts at a birthday cake turned crumbled mess that in no way re-sembled the food blogger's curated photos on the screen. We should laugh at these fails because the stark differences are comical. But in these attempts, we can't forget to call our own versions of creation good. In fact, it would likely do us well not to try to copy because we'll be nothing but disappointed.

In his book *Create vs. Copy,* pastor and author Ken Wytsma says,

> This kind of copying simply takes what is known and safe and repeats it *ad infinitum.*
>
> Creators, on the other hand, do borrow much . . . but for the purpose of making things new. The Renaissance artists of Florence borrowed from Greek myths, humanism, and Roman architecture, but always with the mindset of *transforming*—not merely copying—what had come before.[4]

I may not be transforming architecture, but I am transforming my little circles of influence. I can build on what I know is good and make it my own.

As makers, we make in many ways:

With our hands. Creating in the physical world includes digging in the dirt, sewing on the ribbon, painting on the canvas. No doubt the physical work of our hands has a spiritual component. Jesus was God incarnate—he came in the flesh (not to mention he was a carpenter by trade)—so we know that the embodied life has significance. Whether we're hammering a nail, wrapping a gift, or pruning a rosebush, making what is lovely with our hands is true and beautiful work.

With our minds. Those physical representations must first be conceived of. The engineer has to design the bridge for the construction foreperson to do their job. The excavator must assess the site before beginning the dig. Our imagination combined with our logic and problem-solving skills bring us much of what we make. We also form ideas and opinions. We "make up our minds" based on how and what we think. These are unique processes for each of us. The mind is a beautiful tool that God created for his glory. May we use it for such purposes.

With our words. Whether we sing, write, or say our words, they have power to give life or destroy (Prov. 18:21). God spoke creation into being (Gen. 1). Jesus is the Word made flesh (John 1:14). Words reflect the holy.

AFFIRMATION OF EVERYDAY MAKING

List the ways you make something from nothing during a typical week.

Read your list out loud and call each thing "good."

We can shout or whisper them; we can speak them in our native language or one we've learned from life on this planet. However they are formed, we can choose words of hope or destruction. Words have power.

Beauty for Ashes

That soccer evening sunset, when the sky was an odd and captivating tone of purple with pink and orange streaks, looked like literal paint strokes across the heavens. As had been true for many evenings that fall, the sunset's colors were especially intense because we were viewing them through the veil of record-breaking wildfire smoke. In fact, that night the largest fire in Colorado's history was burning just a few hours from our house.

At the risk of sounding trite or cheesy, I remember that God says he will give us beauty for ashes (Isa. 61:3). He can make beautiful things in place of destruction. It goes back to the arc of creation, separation, reconciliation, and redemption. Most of us haven't experienced fleeing from a wildfire firsthand, but we do know what it feels like to have everything around us burn up. A divorce, job loss, or cancer diagnosis can feel like the collapse of a life. God does not say that he removes the pain; we have to walk through the proverbial fire. But he does say that from the destruction, new things, beautiful things, can grow. These are usually unexpected gifts that were possible only because of the burning down. Does that make the grief any less intense in the moment? No. Can we see God's goodness when this beauty grows and becomes evident in new ways? Yes.

It isn't until we look back that we see God's hand and how he took our pain to create something new, different, and beautiful. Let me be clear, God does not take joy or delight in our pain. He can, however, use anything for something different and good—not immediately, but with time. A new love. A different career path. An unexpected offer of forgiveness and reconciliation. The purple that had never been in our Denver skies was God's new color only because of the fires. "And we know that for those who love God all things work together for good, for those who are called according to his purpose" (Rom. 8:28 ESV).

QUESTIONS TO CONSIDER ABOUT GOD'S BEAUTY FOR ASHES

» When have you felt things falling apart? When has something felt on fire? How did you experience it as it was happening?

» Have you experienced personal growth or transformation as a result? If so, how have you grown? If not, what do you say to God about it?

» How is God's goodness reflected in your ashes? Can you call this new thing beautiful?

» What was your process in being able to see beauty for ashes? How long before you could see it? What does this tell you about God's process and timing?

I've had many moments of clarity in my life when I've been able to see with new eyes how God took something hurtful or destructive and made something new and beautiful from it. I've also had friends give me insight from their observations about my stories and my life. Mentors or just wise people have been able to make connections I'd never seen about one area of life impacting another. Once they made their observation, I could instantly hear the truth and see how God had redeemed a pain point in ways I hadn't previously recognized. When I have made these connections, I've become overwhelmingly grateful for God's mercy and the gentle and gracious ways he has healed hurts with such subtlety. In fact, many times the growing pains happen on the front end, in the burning down, so that as new life is growing I don't notice how much I am changing.

God Has Not Left Us: The Mystery Remains

"Mom, the Trinity is confusing." Eleven-year-old Gracelynn stated what those who have pursued the Christian faith have found true for centuries. And so I did as any good parent would: I attempted to explain in tween terms the mystery of all mysteries while driving home from a pumpkin patch.

It is human nature to want to make sense of our world in concrete terms that we can understand. People seek out religion to explain the larger questions of life, so the tenets need to be clear. Yet I don't have life because of religion. I have life because God made it so. As much as I try to understand who God is and who I am in relation to him, I will never really grasp it. That is not meant to be defeating but an encouragement that none of us have the answers.

Have we lost a little of the mystery of our faith? Have we theologized to death? Have we debated the questions until there is no room left for the uncertain? Have we lost the wonder about the world? Sometimes I'm afraid I've tried to explain away the compelling mystery. I have pursued the logical at the cost of the lovely. I haven't allowed the beautiful to speak for itself even though its truth is obvious. Wonder is lovely.

Christianity is founded on a lot of unlikelies, most of all God coming in human form, dying a physical death, and returning to life. And how about our prayers being heard? The Holy Spirit's work? The virgin birth? You name any of the Christian tenets and you can see how they seem untenable. And yet there is something in my soul that understands there is truth in the gospel. It is the inexplicable quickening that happens when I consider the majesty that is God, the mercy that is Jesus, and the power that is the Holy Spirit. Is there much I don't know? Of course—it's a million times more than what I do know, and this is where faith comes in. I ask God to help me know as much as I need and understand as much as I can and trust that the unknown parts are not to be my concern.

As we search for what is good, we allow ourselves to sit in the lovely, knowing much of what we are seeking out will remain a mystery. That makes it no less true or beautiful.

A Prayer for
WHATEVER IS LOVELY

Oh God, you made it all.
The twinkling lights in the sky,
The cherry blossoms on the ends of every branch,
The dimples in our cheeks,
And the voice of the meadowlark singing its song.

Everything we know of beauty comes from you.
The way our bodies process food for energy and sound
  for language,
The way our hearts burst with pride and our courage
  pushes us down new and unexpected paths,
The way life is born from darkness and leaves again for
  eternity.
It is all from your hand that the good things come.

Give us new eyes to see what you have made.
Give us words to say how your creation is good.
Give us focus to notice the exponential miracles laid out
  on the red carpet of our days.
Give us gratitude to appreciate the gift upon gift that
  comes only from you.

Lord, help us to point out the lovely to others.
The new snow in the driveway that sparkles in the
  morning sun.

The baby's breath in the bouquet that fills in the empty
  spaces,
    And the baby's breath on our chests as we rock new
      life back to sleep.
The refreshment that is forgiveness in a family of
  hardened history,
    And the forgiveness you extend that does not expire.

Lord, we know you make all things new.
Help us to see the way you do.
How you glue back together the shattered clay pots and
  give them new purpose.
You call the cracks beautiful.

May we see the beauty too.
May we see your beauty in every space and place
  through creation or redemption.

In Jesus's name we pray.

Amen.

QUESTIONS *for* REFLECTION

1. Do you sometimes feel the glitter is lost? That you are having a difficult time finding the lovely in your days?

2. How does creation display God's goodness for you? What are two ways you can spend more time outside?

3. How do you do at noticing? What can you do to employ your senses to notice God's goodness?

4. Where can you call out the good that those around you make? How might you encourage other makers?

5. What part of the mystery feels near right now? Where can you sit in the true and beautiful without explaining it?

Surprised by Goodness

Courtney hasn't been a regular churchgoer for a while. Her occasional visits as an adult have been grounded in a bit of curiosity but mostly obligation. She owns her own business and has two little kids. The thought of Sunday church, getting everyone dressed and out of the house on a day off, sounds exhausting on many levels. Coffee, scones, and her Pandora playlist while in her jammies with her family feels more like a relaxing Sunday morning than wrangling kids into car seats, skipping naps, and singing hymns. Not to mention sermons that rarely feel relevant to the family and the business chaos that is her regular life.

But one Sunday morning she found herself sitting alone in her car in a church parking lot, waiting to go in. Was she avoiding what was inside? Maybe a little. Or maybe she was just enjoying the silence and momentary lack of responsibility. Her mom, on staff at this particular church, had just graduated from seminary and was being ordained. Courtney couldn't miss this milestone. Even though she was feeling church wasn't for her, she was for her mom, and her mom needed her there as part of the celebration. Courtney had left her kids and husband at home. This was one of those obligation moments she just needed to get through.

Sitting in her car, watching the minutes on her dashboard click by, Courtney decided she needed an attitude adjustment. She said a prayer. "Help me see what you want me to see today, God. Help me get something out of this." Maybe it wasn't so much a prayer as a resolve to listen with new ears, observe with new eyes, and recognize that not everything about being in church was bad. At least no one in that moment needed her to carry them, feed them, or clean them up after they'd gone potty. She could appreciate the space in her morning to consider more than her regular to-do list. Courtney grabbed her purse from the passenger seat and walked inside, ready to celebrate her mom's accomplishment.

As she sat in the pew alone, Courtney tried to focus on what was happening around her. It was tempting to think about the groceries that needed to be picked up on the way home or worry how the baby was doing in her absence, but she wondered if there was something here for her, if she should be more attentive. Her mom loved this place, after all.

As Courtney listened to the sermon, she almost felt like she should look around the sanctuary to see who was watching her, because the pastor's words seemed tailored directly to her current challenges. The sermon spoke straight to her. The tips applied directly to her current parenting, her marriage, her attitude. The words felt fresh and relevant. She was getting something out of being there.

The service continued, she celebrated her mom's milestone, and on her way home, she considered how her prayer of "God, give me eyes to see" had changed her perspective. Did her perspective change because of her mental shift? Or did it change because of a holy response to her request? Courtney wasn't sure and didn't know if it mattered all that much. What she knew was that she wanted to walk through life looking for the good a little more and seeing how God might be willing to meet her in unexpected places. Even in church.

Part 6

LEADING
with GRACE

Whatever is admirable . . .

PHILIPPIANS 4:8

*When I was a boy and I would see scary things in the
news, my mother would say to me, "Look for the helpers.
You will always find people who are helping."*

FRED ROGERS

Mr. Rogers's famous quote about looking for the
helpers reminds us that in the midst of any crisis
there is usually good to be found. I remember
watching the helpers on my television on September 11,
2001, as firefighters ran into burning towers and later dug
through the rubble. As the footage was on repeat for days,

the world witnessed people-created destruction at its worst and the human spirit at its best. We admire traits like courage and sacrifice over selfishness because we know they are as much discipline as they are instinct. Those who run toward the fire and gunfire are admirable, as is anyone who goes toward pain. Whenever we ask, "Where are the helpers?" I think it would also be appropriate to ask, "Where would Jesus be right now?" I almost always picture Jesus walking toward, standing next to, or leaning into the pain. Jesus walked toward people. He especially walked toward hurting people.

There is a cultural shift taking place as a result of the COVID-19 pandemic. We are naming some of the previously unsung heroes around us. Beyond the typical first responders, we are realizing how others' lives make an impact on ours. From grocery store clerks to nursing home aides to long-haul truckers, we are recognizing how other people impact our systems and therefore our lives for good. As Christians, we can lead the charge on this. We value people because we know each one is uniquely created. We can honor the character traits and noble sacrifices made by those around us, no matter how unexpected or surprising the heroes might be. In calling out these everyday warriors and survivors, we are reminding one another how God is uniquely reflected in each of us.

When we look at The Message interpretation of Philippians 4:8, we see that *admirable* is paraphrased as "gracious." That sounds refreshing, doesn't it? To be gracious people means we are kind and not out to get those around us or catch them doing things they shouldn't. By choice we are highlighting what is good in others. I'd say being gracious is indeed admirable. If something is gracious, it reflects God's grace, showing his divine love that doesn't fixate on the wrongs but extends love anyway. All the blessings he has extended to us are the gracious made tangible. Going back to James 1:17, which says, "Every good gift and every perfect gift is from above" (ESV), we remember that God's goodness is reflected in all that we have that is good. Perhaps that is a good starting place—to remember where God has been gracious.

Gratitude for His Grace

God is gracious to us. That is the cornerstone of our faith. Because of Christ, we get God's grace rather than the consequences of our sin or what we deserve. We go back to that big story pattern of creation, separation, reconciliation, and redemption. His grace reconciles us to him, drawing us closer so that we might experience redemption. That is true for our souls as well as our circumstances and relationships. We cannot escape the pattern of creation and separation built into this world. But if we actively seek his grace, reconciliation, and redemption, we will receive it.

In Matthew 7:7–8, Jesus reminds us that if we come looking for him, we will find him. "Keep on asking, and you will receive what you ask for. Keep on seeking, and you will find. Keep on knocking, and the door will be opened to you. For everyone who asks, receives. Everyone who seeks, finds. And to everyone who knocks, the door will be opened" (NLT). It is with this confidence that we know God is available to us. We can seek out his goodness and find it. That is gracious of him. He does not have to offer us this kindness, and yet he does. The same is true of his grace in our lives. Over and over we choose the path of the fall. We make decisions based on pride, the displaced self-importance that leads us to act as if we are the center of the world. And yet his grace is offered again and again.

This is good news. In fact, it is *the* Good News for humanity. It is from here that we Jesus followers live with gratitude. We are grateful for God-breathed life here on earth, for our numbered days that only he knows, and for life everlasting from glory to glory. If we live in the knowledge of and the experience of God's grace, we naturally live out of gratitude. It is healthy for us to periodically stop and remember how God's grace, his unmerited favor, has been evident in our lives.

The Practice of Gratitude

Derek's work at Providence Network allows me to hear stories of gratitude. Many of the residents at "Prov," as we call it in our house, are in recovery from substance addiction. If you've hit the proverbial rock bottom, you recognize the blessing of a second, third, or fortieth chance. The faith of men and women who have known what it is to fall but then be picked up by grace has been an inspiration to Derek and me. Their daily gratitude for things we take for granted like food and shelter is obvious, but the joy that comes from knowing God's love gives them a certain radiance. We can see someone physically change as they move toward health. Sleep, nutritious food, and safety will do that to a body. But there is also the very unscientific yet undeniable sparkle in a person's eye that comes from a life reborn.

REMEMBERING HIS GRACIOUSNESS

List the ways you have received God's grace

» In the last week:

_____

_____

_____

_____

» In the last month:

_____

_____

_____

_____

» In the last year:

_____

_____

_____

_____

» In your lifetime:

Go through your list and thank God for his gracious provision and love.

God gives us his goodness in the form of hope, laughter, trust, and community. These are his gracious gifts to us, and they give us a meaningful life. As a Christ follower, I see these gifts originating from him. I also believe he can generously give them to people who don't recognize him as Savior. He is gracious and generous that way. So as we witness the transformation of people around us, we can thank God for his gracious provision.

For the residents in the Providence Network community, I see how gratitude stems out of God's grace. They are grateful for provisions I look past or ignore, those things I take for granted. I work at being grateful; sometimes I need to work harder than other times because I easily slip into unconscious entitlement.

When I'm practicing gratitude, it helps to go to the basics. Here's a little of what my starter list looks like when I consider how God has been gracious to me:

A body that works. More specifically, eyes that still see. Knees that bend. Ears to hear the clamor of a full house or crowded car. A brain that sometimes remembers names and works hard to craft coherent sentences. All are gifts that I haven't earned.

A family that loves me. We're a group of imperfect people. We get things wrong. Sometimes we say things really wrong. But our underlying foundation is love for each other. I'm grateful for a faithful spouse and four healthy, full-term babies who are growing into thoughtful, kind young women. I didn't deserve to have four healthy children any more than anyone else, and yet, today I do. I'm grateful for my in-laws and my own mother, who feed us and gift us with resources and time and attention. I take none of these for granted. They are God's grace manifested through people.

A home. I live in a place that gets very cold in the winter. I also know people who have spent nights, years even, on my city's streets. Every time I pull in my driveway, I'm grateful we have an address to come home to. Every below-freezing evening that I open the back door to let the dog in one last time and feel the icy air hit me, I remember it is because of God's grace that I'm on the inside of that doorway. I'm also grateful for things I use that are truly extras— kitchen gadgets, multiple chairs to choose from, doors to close to keep bedrooms quiet.

Grace itself. I want to do things well. Really well. I perhaps fall under the perfectionist umbrella. You'd

191

never know it by looking at the state of my home, but that's because I get paralyzed by projects that I'm afraid I'm going to do "wrong." Inactivity is often the result of perfection paralysis. Guess what? God's grace says I'm free from this kind of performance-based living. The only problem is that my self-created, unrealistic expectations get in the way of the freedom offered through grace. I have nothing to measure up to. God is expecting nothing but gratitude in exchange for his grace.

Once I start naming specific ways God has been gracious to me, my radar goes up and I start becoming grateful for the less obvious. Clean, running water—yes, I'm grateful for this. Hot water—such a bonus. Two showers to choose from in our home? Pure luxury. When the drains get clogged with hair and the plastic shower curtain liner looks mildewy, I come back to the basics. Warm, clean water in our house is a gift that I didn't earn. I know not every woman in the

GRATITUDE FOR THE LESS OBVIOUS

Consider the previous list you made about how God has been gracious to you. What gifts did you miss? What else can you thank him for? Go back and add to your list.

world has access to this. God has been gracious in this area of my life. God's grace becomes clearly evident, and my gratitude is amplified with every detail I notice. All these specifics further show me what is good.

When We Are Gracious, We Find What Is Admirable

Lisa knew that her new coworker, Tammy, wasn't happy. Lisa had just been hired. She was part of a new group of people brought in after a company takeover, and Tammy made it clear that Lisa represented all that was wrong with their now shared employer. They worked closely together for hours every day, often the only ones in the office. As uncomfortable as it was, it was impossible to avoid each other. They had no choice but to show up in the morning and make it work.

From the outside you would expect some disconnect between these two women. Lisa was young, married, and generally optimistic. What she lacked in experience she made up for in enthusiasm. Tammy was past the midpoint of her life and lived alone. Lisa was determined to show Tammy that she appreciated her loyalty to the company, so she shifted her enthusiasm into dependability and vowed to consistently be a positive coworker.

Time and consistency did their work, and soon the frigid tension between them began to thaw. Lisa could more easily see Tammy's qualities that made her a good employee, and Tammy felt less threatened by Lisa's presence. The change wasn't immediate, and it took two willing parties to see what was admirable in each other. This was a developing relationship that could have gone either way: toward mutual appreciation or increased mistrust.

It wasn't long after her arrival that Lisa was pregnant and very sick. Her pregnancy developed some complications, and she needed to leave work frequently for doctors' appointments. This didn't help the consistency with Tammy, but Lisa offered updates as she returned from each appointment. Lisa was stressed and Tammy listened.

Because of the baby's irregular in utero heart pattern, Lisa couldn't have any caffeine or chocolate during the later end of her pregnancy. One day Tammy brought ginger candies to the office. She remembered something Lisa had mentioned months earlier about liking them. Tammy's memory of such a specific detail caught Lisa off guard. It made her realize how closely Tammy was listening to her. In fact, Tammy knew more about Lisa's pregnancy concerns than many of Lisa's close friends. Their proximity and daily contact, along with Lisa's push forward and Tammy's willingness to reciprocate, led to friendship—two people in mutual like with each other. Again, this didn't happen instantly but rather in the gracious rhythm of each woman continually looking for the best in the other until that became their natural instinct.

Isn't that what we all want? To lead with the ability to see what is admirable in others? But that isn't always our automatic bent, either because of our own personality or because of the challenges others throw our way. Usually our hesitation in leading with grace is a combination of both.

So how do we follow Lisa and Tammy's lead here? We can see a few things they did right.

They moved past their roles. Both women had their assigned duties they were being paid to complete.

They could have focused on what was required of them by their job descriptions and gone no further in their relationship, but that would have maintained a miserable work environment. They chose to learn about each other beyond their defined co-working roles.

They listened to each other. It's one thing to hear the information someone is giving you; it's another to remember the details in order to better care for the person. The ginger candies were a symbolic representation of Tammy caring for Lisa. This couldn't have happened without Tammy really listening and considering how she could take care of her officemate.

They chose the better. There were daily opportunities both to get annoyed with each other and to see each other's admirable qualities. Over the course of their year working together, they chose the better. Were there hard moments? I'm sure, yes. But they were able to move past the smaller annoyances and choose the better in the larger scope of things. The better work environment. The better service to each other, to their employer, and to their clients. Everyone benefited because they were gracious and sought out the good.

They cared for each other. Two women who might not have been friends had they not been working in such close quarters cared for each other in real time. Tammy listened as Lisa reported on her multiple doctors' appointments and her fears connected to the high-risk nature of the pregnancy. Lisa appreciated how good Tammy was at her job and encouraged her as she faced the challenges of new management. Had they worked together at a different time, they wouldn't have had the unique opportunities to care through the distinct challenges that particular year presented in both of their lives.

Most of us find ourselves in relationships with people we don't choose—family, coworkers, neighbors, teachers, churchgoers. When we are gracious, assuming the best in others before jumping to the worst, we tend to find friends in unexpected places. We all have our quirks. Let's go into every new relationship with that understanding and lead with grace to find what is admirable.

Believing the Best in Each Other

In a cultural moment defined by actively seeking out the worst and calling it out, we as Christ followers can (and should) offer a different mode of operation. We can actively work at seeking out the best. With some people it's easy. We genuinely like them. Their personalities sparkle. Their hearts are generous and anything but self-serving. They ask us to coffee or for an after-work drink, and we think it's a really good idea. It's easy to find the best in this crowd.

Then there are the people we pretend we don't see when we're at the pharmacy. We know they are made in God's image, but we have a hard time liking them in the moment. They grate on us for different reasons. They talk too much or not enough. Their sense of humor hits us as off or their personality as odd. We disagree with their tone or their politics or their general worldview. They have their fans (we hope), but we aren't them. That's the honest approach.

Now we go for the admirable approach. We look for what is good and honorable in those hard-to-love people, and we celebrate what is best instead of fixating on what we see as their worst. We pull out the very good attributes and name them.

Parents have been doing this since the beginning of time. We are wired to see what is good in our wacky, often unlikable children and call it out. We are also wired to turn what may be considered a less-than-desirable attribute into something to celebrate. So let's think as parents for a moment as we consider what it is to believe the best in someone. It may help us to see a fellow person as God does. We are looking for what is underneath. I think of this as their foundation as a person. Those quirks and details that might drive us a bit bonkers are the accessories. Here are some things we can look for to find the good, true, and beautiful even when the grating happens:

Passion. Too much talk in a direction you don't agree with or about a topic you just have no interest in? I've heard people say, "They talked about cooking! For an hour!" One person's boring is another's interesting. Appreciate the person's passion for the subject matter. It may inspire you in a new area, or at least in another area you find interesting.

Consistency. Is the person always negative? Late? Ready with a comeback? It doesn't matter the habit; if it annoys you and it happens frequently, you can appreciate that person's consistency. Thinking of it through this lens could make you smile and say the next time it happens: "At least she's consistent."

Motives. Almost everyone I know who disagrees with me has wonderful motives; we just don't come to the same conclusions about solutions or approaches. Consider someone's motivation for why or how they do something, and suddenly you're able to be a little more gracious without even forcing it.

Skill set. Your personalities may not meld well, but you can appreciate someone's excellence in their work. It always helps to list off someone's talents—maybe not out loud but to yourself—as you consider what you appreciate. Any natural talent or any skill that takes a lot of time to develop can be appreciated, especially if it's one that is not commonplace.

Commitment. A combination of consistency and motives, commitment is a wonderful trait in a person. Whether you're both in the office or on the school fundraising committee, you can often find common ground with this person if you are committed to the same goal. Or simply notice their commitment to their cause, family, or cubicle cleanliness. Commitment alone is a rare trait in an age when people bolt as soon as things get hard.

Gratitude for others often comes down to being able to find what is admirable. If it takes a little work to get to the naming, that's okay. The goal is working toward seeing the good in one another. It's there for the finding.

FINDING THE BEST IN SOMEONE

» Be honest. Name one person (or ten people) that you have a hard time offering grace to.

» Consider what is underneath and where you might be gracious.

» Name three traits you find admirable in this person.

» Ask the Holy Spirit to give you a filter to see what is best before you find what is worst in this person.

Being Gracious on Social Media

I sat at my keyboard, my fingers pecking out my response with rapid speed. I should have known through the force of each punch of the key that the energy I was feeling around this conversation was not positive (a slight understatement). The person on the other side of the screen had not only offended my personal stance on the issue of the day; she had also dismissed every faithful woman I knew who believed as I did. I couldn't just let the comment go. I needed to stand up for my people! Unlike when I was feeling canceled, the post was not personal or directed at me, but I took it that way. We can all be tempted to read more into a social media post than is intended.

Not surprisingly, my response was less than gracious. I went from defense mode to attack mode. So, as I've done many times before, I deleted the comment before I published it. The problem with social media is we are interacting with a screen rather than a person sitting across the desk or the room. We say things with our fingers we would never say in person because they are too hurtful. We feel an unhealthy permission to get nastier than we would if we had to look the other person in the eye to say our comment. This is a dangerous place to be.

We can avoid participating in social media, as many (like my own husband) have largely done, or we can use it as a tool to convey God's goodness. Both are acceptable responses. If you're participating in these online platforms but feeling a disconnect between your tone and what you want to convey, consider doing one of the following (many of these principles work in face-to-face conversations too):

Walk away. If you can't control your emotions in that
   moment, if that "I'm going to show them" feeling
   rises in your chest, put the phone down or close
   your computer and do not comment. Give yourself
   twenty-four hours to step away from the conversation to gain some composure. Saying things out of
   anger or frustration usually isn't productive.

Write your thoughts out somewhere else. Often the exchange of ideas on social media touches a nerve we
   weren't even aware was there. You may have feelings
   and opinions on a subject that you haven't totally
   thought through, but you need to get your words
   out. Great! Maybe the best place to write those
   words is in a journal, a Word document, or a draft
   email. Once they're written, you may be better able
   to articulate how you feel and why in a more public
   space.

Make a commitment to yourself. Having some type of personal litmus test will help you discern where the line
   is when approaching a topic. If your commitment is
   to say only encouraging things, simply ask yourself,
   "Is this encouraging?" Your answer will come pretty
   quickly.

Be mindful of who you follow. As with anything in life,
   what we consume impacts what we put out. If you
   tend to follow (or be friends with, depending on
   the platform) people who have a nasty tone, you
   will unconsciously normalize that behavior. You
   should certainly follow people who think differently
   than you do and hold different worldviews, but they

should be able to convey their ideas with civility and kindness.

Change platforms. Different social media platforms lend themselves to different types of interaction. I use Twitter for sharing news and ideas, often with people I don't actually know. Facebook is my place to tell real-life friends and readers what I'm up to. Instagram lends itself more to the pretty pictures (though that too is evolving). If one site isn't working for you, perhaps a change in platform will help.

Delete past posts or comments. If after reflection you decide you want to make a change in what you previously put into the social world, it is okay to go back and delete things that do not reflect what you currently want to convey. I give you full permission to change for the better. You are not being disingenuous by taking things down; you are improving, and I think that reflects what's true and beautiful.

We have agency in how we use social media. The free will God grants us extends beyond our face-to-face relationships to how we respond in the virtual world. If you want to do better in this area, you can and will be more likely to leave the aroma of Christ if you center on grace and kindness.

The Power of "I Wonder"

My friend Krista recently asked me what I would do in a contentious discussion where I disagreed with the other person to the point that it made me uncomfortable and I questioned if my silence would indicate agreement. Would

I let it slide? What if it felt too important to ignore? Would I confront the person or challenge their thinking outright? What if it put the relationship at risk? Would I be willing to do that? These are all valid questions, especially in light of being gracious and looking for the best in other people.

How can we be gracious when we feel strongly about something and the other person is just not able to see things our way? We can fight back. This tactic is sometimes called for, but it's often not effective. When we go into fight mode, people feel defensive, and their listening and learning tend to shut down. When we're going on the attack, our physical bodies are responding with tension and adrenaline, looking for a way to release them. At this deciding moment of how to respond, may I offer the power of "I wonder"? Put down the pointer finger (literal and proverbial), take a deep breath, and say, "I wonder . . ."

"I wonder how this impacts Dan in the office next to us."

"I wonder what Margie down the street would think of this."

"I wonder what unintended consequences might pop up for our students."

"I wonder" takes the conflict away from "you against me" in a disagreement and becomes an invitation to consider the problem together. How does this approach help us be gracious? We are offering a way outside of conflict. We are taking the false dichotomy and turning it on its head to say, "Maybe it's neither this nor that; maybe it's something we haven't yet thought of together." It also creates space for empathy as we wonder together how something may impact someone outside of the conversation. Often in conflict we ground ourselves on sides—my side versus your side. "I wonder" removes that binary approach and asks, *What about my neighbor? How am I my brother's keeper right now? Where would Jesus be looking and standing in this situation?*

To be gracious is to make it not about those of us in the conversation but about the momentum of where God is at work. It is stepping outside of our immediate agenda and asking—wondering, if you will—what God's agenda is for the larger circle of his creation. "I wonder" is disarming; it helps us put our weapons of accusation down. I can't think of anything more gracious than that.

Saying (Out Loud) What Is Good

People feel loved, noticed, and cherished when someone speaks truth into their hearts. After all, God made his creation, including us, good. He named what he saw. And we want to hear that we are doing well. There are entire parenting philosophies on praising what children are doing right rather than fixating on what they are doing wrong. My mom's dog trainer applies this principle, and HR executives give strengths-based goals and evaluations as employee motivators. To say people like being told what they're good at and where they're doing things right is an understatement. We run toward that kind of praise.

It all comes down to our desire to have words of love spoken to us. We want what is good in us to be reflected back to us. And we can give that gift to one another with a gracious tone.

I'll confess that my words can be harsh. In the spirit of "honesty" or being "realistic," I can easily be the Debbie Downer and call out what could be improved. Usually I'm not intending to be critical, I'm just pointing out the weak spots. It's a helpful trait in emergency planning but not as helpful in nurturing relationships. There is a time for critical thinking and even critical speaking, but it turns out I don't have to work on those. I give them out in bigger doses than is helpful sometimes. I do need to work on calling out the good with equal measure—to say it out loud, write it down. If I appreciate things about other people and don't tell them, I'm inching toward taking people for granted.

Following are a few ways you can actively call out the good in someone else:

> *If you think something nice, say it.* "I like how that looks on you." "Wow, you're really good at that." "You are so generous." "I felt supported when you said that in the meeting earlier." You know the old saying, "If you can't say something nice, don't say anything at all"? The opposite is also generally true: "If you can say something nice, say it." In a world where people are torn down left and right, calling good out in someone is like breathing life back into them.

> *Be specific.* "I appreciate how you talked to your sister when you were both angry. You showed kindness and forgiveness with your words" is more effective than "You were nice to your sister." First, it helps the other person know exactly what you appreciated about that moment. Second, receiving a genuine,

specific compliment like that resonates in a different way than a general one because the person feels seen. They know someone noticed what they were working toward.

Pray for new eyes. We find what we look for. If we want to see the good in someone else so we can call it out and reflect it back to them, we sometimes need a different kind of vision. Ask God to help you see what he sees. Ask the Holy Spirit to be a lens of love that illuminates what is good so you and others can admire it.

Celebrating What Is Admirable

The good in the world deserves to be recognized in a public way. We collectively need to recognize a person's contribution, effort, or accomplishment. But not everyone likes an award or a bonus check (okay, probably most people like a bonus). Some would prefer a small gathering to a big one or time with people rather than a gift. Others would like just the opposite.

Perhaps you know it's time to celebrate someone, to mark his or her contribution to the world or group, but you don't know how to make it meaningful. Do you just do another cake in the office break room? Send them a card? Buy them their favorite coffee drink? That might feel predictable or uncreative to one person but extremely thoughtful to another. How do we know how to best celebrate those around us? How do we say their qualities or accomplishments are admirable in a way that feels personal and meaningful to the one being celebrated? It takes a little bit of intentionality.

Karen works with Derek at Providence Network. As part of her role as the COO of their small nonprofit, she is in charge of the official staff celebrations. It is clear to everyone that Karen would take on the role of celebration coordinator even if it wasn't in her job description because she is great at recognizing people in a way that is meaningful to them. I can send someone a card or buy a gift because I think I should, but Karen does some investigating into what the person to be honored would like.

Karen wanted to throw a party for Derek's ten-year anniversary with the organization. She knew how much he hated being the center of attention and would not look forward to any kind of gathering in his honor, but she also thought it was important to collectively and publicly celebrate him. So she planned a surprise party because he wouldn't have time to dread it. When she called me with the idea, I knew she was absolutely right—Derek would hate knowing there was a party headed his way, and he would benefit from it in the end. Karen's solution was just right.

From parties to gifts, Karen considers a person's preferences and personality when deciding how to mark an accomplishment or an effort that's worth celebrating. Here are some of Karen's tips:

Words. Some people love to hear why others appreciate them. This could be in a toast or a note. Remember the more specific, the better. Karen's tip: "The written word is always appreciated. A letter or card (given the rarity of personal mail) or one of my favorites: a small decorative box (that suits them) filled with words of affirmation by those who know them well . . . which allows the whole group to participate."

Tangible gifts. Karen's tip: "When it's a special life event or accomplishment, a gift is a nice way to memorialize it. Depending on their situation and interests, make it one that serves a practical need *or* that involves an activity they would enjoy and may not otherwise spend the money to do. In the right circumstances, personalizing it (names, dates, photos, messages) makes it unique to *them*."

The gift of time. Karen's tip: "For those who seemingly have or have done everything, a gift of time (alone or with others) can be a creative option, especially if you package it in a festive way. It's all about the presentation." When I think of quality time, I think of people being together. But Karen points out that quality time can also mean time as a gift for someone to spend however they want. A free day? I'll take it!

Meeting a need. Karen's personal favorite: "To me, 'honoring' also relates to recognizing/addressing a need (another set of hands, an errand, a meal) or the person's existence (a new neighbor). People are often reluctant to make the first move or ask for help, which makes our response to a need that much sweeter." How can we be offering people help in a way that will actually be helpful and where it's not awkward for them to say yes?

I noticed Karen's themes loosely followed Gary Chapman's popular book *The 5 Love Languages.* The premise is we can give and receive love in a variety of ways. We all have a few "languages" that feel especially meaningful to us but may not matter to someone else (some people are huggers; others aren't). Karen agreed that she loosely uses the concepts in *The 5 Love Languages* as a guide to help her think through what would be most meaningful to someone else. The key is, she does the research to learn what will indeed speak to a person and plans the celebration with that person in mind.

This kind of intentional sleuthing is not only helpful but also fun! We get to tell other people they are appreciated in a way that they can hear clearly.

God rejoices over us. He delights in us. And we can do this for one another as a tangible reminder that when he made us, his creation, God called us good.

CELEBRATING WITH INTENTION

» Who in your life needs to be celebrated?
» In what ways does this person feel loved? What's their "love language"?
» How can you incorporate those ways into a group celebration?
» Make a plan now for how you will celebrate someone in the coming week.

God Has Not Left Us: We See Good in Each Other

You've likely known that person, the one who is always glad to see you. Maybe it's been a grandparent or a teacher, or perhaps a pastor or a friend at work. They stop what they are doing when you arrive, or at least it feels that way, and give you their full attention. This person has seen the good in you. Sometimes they articulate it back to you, saying things like "You're so good at that," or they simply delight in who you are, asking question after question and hanging on your every word. They make you feel like you have something to offer the world and that they are better for knowing you.

My friend Rachel's mom, Linda, was like this. She would visit us in our off-campus college house and take us out to dinner. I felt interesting and valued when I was with her (talk about a confidence boost) because she listened without distraction and then affirmed with her words the good she saw in me. I felt loved.

As an adult, I've thought of Linda often. She wasn't known just in our college friends' circle as the cheerleader mom; she also had a reputation in her small town of knowing and loving people well. I've asked myself, *What was it about her that made people feel so special?* She welcomed and celebrated. She accepted people exactly as they were. She didn't fixate on places where they could do better—she probably assumed they knew those spots already—but she called out where they were doing things right. She was gracious and saw what was good.

I don't know how naturally this came to Linda and how much was an intentional decision on her part to respond to people that way. My guess is it was a combination of the two. That gives me hope that even if (okay, even when) I don't have the automatic response of calling out the good, I can use my agency and discipline to choose to do a better job. Once again I think of where Jesus would be standing in conversations, what his message to people would be, and I get the sense he would want people to know first that they are loved. Because when we know we're loved, we're in a much better position to turn to the people around us and offer a little grace.

I remember the last time I saw Linda before she died. I had my two older girls with me. They were still little, and she met me right where I was in that stage of life. Though she was battling cancer, she focused the conversation around me. She affirmed my mothering and made me feel like she always did, like I was the most important person in the room. Whenever I remember her, I think, *I want to be more like Linda.* When I get to the heart of that, it's because Linda was an incredible reflection of Jesus.

A Prayer for
WHATEVER IS ADMIRABLE

Lord, we confess we look for the wrong,
    The places we disagree,
    Our differences,
    And our sticking points.

We forget to look at each other with fresh eyes,
    To see where you are already evident
    In the work ethic,
    The generous gestures,
    The consistency of character.

We are the opposite of gracious as we
    Point out the holes,
    Nitpick our lives apart,
    And focus in on the hard,
        to the point that we forget to see the good.

Jesus, we know you stand with us kitchen
    anthropologists as we stand in our places, looking out
    our windows at the world.

Lord, may our tongues be hesitant to rattle off criticism
And willing to sing each other's praises.
May we extend grace where graciousness is called for.
May we show admiration where it is deserved.

*May we model the hearts and thoughts you'd like us to,
reflecting your goodness back to the world.*

*May we not take anything or anyone for granted
But rather celebrate how and why people and places are
reflections of you.*

In Jesus's name we pray.

Amen.

QUESTIONS *for* REFLECTION

1. What traits do you find admirable? How can you more intentionally recognize and call out those traits in others?

2. Where can you apply "I wonder" in your conversations? How might doing so help you lead with grace?

3. How has social media use impacted your ability to see the good in others? Are there any consumption habits you should change?

4. How do you feel most celebrated? (There are no wrong answers.)

5. Who has seen the best in you and made you feel loved? What specifically did they do to make you feel that way? How can you mirror those behaviors?

Believing the Best in Each Other

It was a Sunday afternoon before a big national election, and Jon's family was doing what many do on the weekend—they were sitting around his in-laws' house, laughing at kids, and sharing some food and drink. The election was filling the headlines, but politics wasn't something this extended family often covered in conversation. Everyone knew there were political differences in their circle, and out of respect for each other and maybe a dose of wanting to avoid conflict, it was just something that wasn't talked about. Until this Sunday afternoon.

Jon was sitting with his father-in-law, Mike, who surprised him by asking outright why he supported a given presidential candidate. Right away Jon was struck by the tone in his father-in-law's voice: it was one of genuine curiosity. Jon knew Mike to be a compassionate man. A pastor, Mike was naturally bent toward being curious about people's beliefs and ideas. Jon also suspected he wasn't supporting the same candidate. And so they talked.

You know what? It went really well. Why? Because these two men entered the conversation believing the best in each other. They weren't interested in shaming or having a "gotcha" comeback. They were truly interested in learning. Jon later reflected that Mike never cut him off or tried to discredit Jon's points but rather asked follow-up questions. They both knew the other person cared about people, about the country, and about how people care for each other.

Naturally the presidential candidate discussion moved them into specific policy topics: abortion, LGBTQ+ rights, universal health care, and taxes were all covered. In other words, they hit some heavy issues. "We agreed that there was a role for government in our society," Jon reflected. "That was our common ground, our starting place, to then move out and talk specifics about what exactly government involvement in society looked like."

Jon and Mike weren't having this conversation in a vacuum. They have been in a relationship for more than sixteen years. Their history of trust was a foundation for them to enter the conversation well. They also had a future together, meaning neither wanted to say anything that they would later regret. Both words and tone were considered as they presented their ideas, asked questions, and listened to each other, because maintaining a respectful posture was key to the long-term health of their relationship.

"I knew my father-in-law to be a compassionate man," Jon said. "So I tailored our conversation toward his compassion, asking, 'What would be the compassionate response in these various scenarios?'"

Jon not only believed the best in his father-in-law but also spoke to and appealed to his best. He thought on what was admirable about him and built on that. Jon would say Mike did the same. They went into the conversation seeking good, believing it was there, and used that belief to reflect their decent and good qualities back to each other. They sought what was true and beautiful, found it, called it out, and reflected it back.

What could have been a contentious argument was a productive discussion because two men looked for common ground in a conversation where they knew there would be disagreement.

They depended on their mutual trust to carry them forward into uncharted territory. They listened intently, acknowledging when the other person made an interesting or new point they hadn't previously considered, and they took the labeling of "good person" or "bad person" off the table because they already believed each other to be good. There was the option in every step of this process to lean toward either mutual care or mutual disdain. In a lengthy discussion, there are many opportunities to eye roll, sigh, accuse, or add a sarcastic comment. These men chose over and over to believe the best in each other instead of the worst, and their body language, tone of voice, and word choice demonstrated that.

The conversation ended as many family events do. Jon's two toddlers started melting down, and it was time to leave the grandparents' house and head home for naps. Although Jon and Mike talked through some hot-button issues in a more candid way than they'd ever done before, they were able to walk away feeling like they understood each other better.

That is the joy of seeking out the good in someone else. When you go looking for it, you usually find it.

CONCLUSION

God has not left us

If anything is excellent or praiseworthy . . .

PHILIPPIANS 4:8

It never hurts to keep looking for sunshine.

EEYORE

I am sitting again in my home office, an early morning right before dawn. Outside my window I see my neighbor's dark tree branches against the bluish purple of the first light appearing. It is stormy outside, and the branches are moving side to side with the leaves barely hanging on. As the light starts to brighten, I know that the tree stands between me and the sunrise. I have to look through the pattern of branches and leaves to see the beauty of the changing sky.

The tree is an obstacle in my view, and yet it is also the framework by which I can see the gift that is this morning's sunrise. My praise in this moment is that the sun exists, it is rising, I know about it, and I can see it even though my view is obstructed. The formation of the tree and its contrast against the now purply-pink sky give the light a texture that I can see and understand only from where I'm sitting. Though millions of people around the metro area have the opportunity to look east toward the horizon at this moment to see the sun rising, few are (it is early morning, after all), and no one can see it from my exact vantage point, with this particular tree as the sunrise's frame.

So it is with our faith journey. No one else will hear the gospel with the exact same tone and meaning as I do because no one else has my exact vantage point. As I watch the sky continue to brighten, the branches blowing in the wind, I am struck by this gift of a sunrise that is both universal and personal. Everyone in Denver has access to it—God does not offer the sunrise for only a few. And I am the only one who has this view of it.

We can remember this as we seek out goodness in the world. God offers many gifts to all of us, yet we receive them differently. He offers mountain ranges and dandelion poufs and raccoons for us to enjoy. He offers finger joints and imaginations and taste buds to nearly all of us, yet we experience them in our unique ways. We can pray, worship, and read Scripture and have different experiences and understandings because God is dynamic and meets us in our distinct needs.

When we think on what is praiseworthy, we naturally think on God and his majesty. We can also know that those around us will experience his goodness uniquely. We are fallible people. We cannot achieve perfection, but we can strive for excellence and celebrate it when we see it in others. Jesus called out goodness in others, and we can too. We can also work to maintain a standard of excellence in the things we do, not because we want approval but because we believe if God has called us to something (a job, task, ministry), it must be worth doing well. We can be generous with our praise and lavish with our cheerleading because God does not hold back his loving generosity from us. Why not be people known for giving our best to our work and to one another? This generosity of spirit, this calling out of goodness, this dependable grace, will be the enticing aroma of Jesus that many will be drawn to.

If Anything Is Praiseworthy

In all things give praise. That's what we're taught as Christians, and rightly so. First Thessalonians 5:16–18 says, "Rejoice always, pray continually, give thanks in all circumstances; for this is God's will for you in Christ Jesus." When grief comes, the phone call brings bad news, the job loss is unexpected, and the infertility moves from months to years long, we hardly want to give praise. Yet we have Christ. It is not Christ's will for us to suffer, but it is his will for us to find joy in the midst of what can be a very difficult life. I've never been a fan of the phrase "Life is good" because life in various moments can feel very, very bad. And yet life found in hope in Christ is always good. This is the paradox of the Christian faith. We can hate our circumstances and rejoice in them at the same time.

The gospel is *the* Good News. The good news for all people in all times. Yes, in all circumstances. It is another paradox that this good news is equally good no matter the suffering. In fact, it can be even more of a relief the deeper the grief. The Good News itself reflects this pain-praise contrast. Christ had to die in order for the resurrection to occur. Creation. Separation. Reconciliation. Redemption. The separation, the fall, is part of the process. The fall is all things that are not as they should be. All things that grieve us. All things that remind us that the opposite of good exists in this world. But then comes the reconciliation. We draw closer to God when our pain points are strongest. So though he does not endorse or plan or create our pain, he does not abandon us when we experience it.

This is when we can push toward hope, or in many cases collapse into it from exhaustion, despair, and darkness that feels it will never lift. He is already where our grief takes us. No matter how we arrive at our pain, he is waiting. This reconciliation can be a life-changing event, but for most of us our daily turning toward hope is the more common practice. I can experience this reconciliation daily, sometimes in the same set of circumstances as yesterday or a million yesterdays, sometimes in new ones. Sometimes in life-altering grief but also in minor annoyances. He is waiting for me to turn to him and give thanks for *him*. This is the continual prayer process that leads us to "rejoice always."

We rejoice because God is good in all things. He is good on his own. Our pain does not fuel his goodness. In other words, he does not need us to experience heartache in this life. However, our pain can be used as a tool to reconcile us with him. It involves some choice on our part to turn

REJOICE ALWAYS

» Choose an act you do multiple times a day that doesn't require your attention. It could be walking into a different room, picking up your phone, or opening the fridge door.

» Choose one area of your life where you are struggling. It could be a relationship, a source of work stress, or a health issue.

» Every time you perform your rote activity, thank God for his continued goodness in the middle of your struggle. Have it be a simple prayer: "Lord, thank you." "God, your goodness does not end." "Be still and know."

toward him to accept his tender mercies and care. It will not eliminate our grief, but it may make it bearable. We are finding the good that has not left us when we focus on what is praiseworthy.

Seeing in the Fog

We don't yet see things clearly. We're squinting in a fog, peering through a mist. But it won't be long before the weather clears and the sun shines bright! We'll see it all then, see it all as clearly as God sees us, knowing him directly just as he knows us!

But for right now, until that completeness, we have three things to do to lead us toward that consummation: Trust steadily in God, hope unswervingly, love extravagantly. And the best of the three is love. (1 Cor. 13:12–13 MSG)

When I think of fog, I picture my childhood in the Pacific Northwest, where late fall days were marked with low-lying clouds and a mist that reached down to the damp sidewalks and lush lawns. Walking on Seattle's streets, there was a chill with the moisture, which I don't feel now in arid Denver, even on our occasional rainy days. Though it was cold, the misty fog felt refreshing. It also felt mysterious, and sometimes as the seasonal affect settled in, it felt depressing. I had a sense of wanting to hunker down, get back inside, and make another cup of coffee.

Often on those walks in the fog, whether on a trail, down my own street, or along the beach, I could not see what was ahead. But even though I couldn't see, I knew something was there. Sometimes I knew because it was familiar territory that I'd walked or driven down hundreds of times. I could say with certainty what was in the distance. If it was a new place, I often couldn't tell you the details of what was ahead, whether shops or turns in the trail, but I knew that the world didn't just end beyond what I could see.

There are many parts of life where the path has not been laid out clearly. Where the fog of uncertainty limits our vision of what's ahead. A diagnosis. A career path. A child in crisis. We can only see what is right in front of us. The bends in the road are not evident until we get closer, and then we can see just beyond to the next spot and the next. So it is with our faith. We take steps forward through the fog, and with every step we are able to see that much farther ahead.

We know that God and his goodness are still present. We trust as we walk through life that faith, hope, and love remain even if we can't see them. We keep looking because to find them is great joy. In fact, we are wired to look for, find, and name what is true and beautiful. And so we take that next step, and the next, trusting we will be able to see a bit more of God's goodness ahead. That goodness appears, and as we get closer, we see with more clarity what we trusted was there all along. God has not left us. His goodness is all around us.

A Prayer for
THE PRAISEWORTHY

Lord God, in all things we give praise.
We know these words are often spoken,
But our hearts aren't true to the call.

We dissect what we deem true and beautiful in a
*   situation and call the rest waste.*
We determine what is praiseworthy material and what
*   is not.*
We talk about you, around you, and seldom to you,
Rather than giving you praise in all circumstances.

So right now, Lord, we put down our caveats for just a
*   moment.*
We place our expectations at your feet,
Our exceptions at your throne,
Our overthinking and underbelieving at your cross.

We step past our doubts
Around our overscheduled pace, overspending pride,
*   and overconfident decision-making,*
And we continue toward you.
We allow those old clothes to drop off—
They slow us down with their weight, after all—
And we give you our full selves
For worship.

You alone can give us the hope, satisfaction, and rest we
    scramble so hard
To make happen on our own.
We get creative in our attempts to self-satisfy,
To meet our own needs,
To save ourselves.

And then we feel surprised when that doesn't work.
Again.
And we remember you.
You alone.

We praise you for what you have made that is good,
For your desire to be with us and your action to come,
For your life here on these streets, in these valleys,
And your new life offered moment by moment, forever
    and forever.
We praise you for the death you wore and the comeback
    you made.
We praise you for the witnesses who saw and told from
    that first moment to today.

Jesus in the swaddling clothes, we praise you.
Father in heaven, we praise you.
Spirit who moves among and in and through us, we
    praise you.

Amen.

ACKNOWLEDGMENTS

I will never forget writing this book. A global pandemic. Racial protests. A divisive presidential election. Virtual school the entire time. In some ways it was the best possible point in my life to write about seeking out goodness. God's mercy and goodness were evident even in this.

A special thanks to Teresa Evenson and William K. Jensen Literary Agency for continuing to be my cheerleaders. Teresa, you have become a dear friend and advisor. I appreciate your special encouragement around this book. Thank you to Rebekah Guzman and the Baker Books team for pursuing this. May we together put words in the world that speak of God's goodness.

To my team of readers and consultants I owe an extra dose of gratitude. During your own pandemic lives, you encouraged and read and responded with suggestions, questions, and "I wonders." Colleen Blake-Miller, Allie Smith, Cara Meredith, Annie Rim, Krista Gilbert, Karen Parks,

Derek Kuykendall, Traci Willhite, Karen Huston, Susan Burkholder, Kendra Tillman, Tammy Strait, Maggie John, Shannon Polk, and Carol Kuykendall, you helped make this book what it is.

To my everyday people, my quarantine crew, I love you. God's goodness is evident in you. Thank you for letting me close the office door for hours at a time and for making more coffee. I will always cherish our extended pandemic time together and see it as good in the midst of a lot of hard.

To my readers, if you've picked up this book, I am humbled. I pray it offers you hope no matter your circumstances. Creation. Separation. Reconciliation. Redemption. Your story is always pushing toward redemption.

To God be the glory.

NOTES

Part 1 The Truth, the Whole Truth, and Nothing but the Truth (So Help Me, God)

1. Karl Barth, quoted in "Barth in Retirement," *Time*, May 31, 1963, 59.

Part 2 Canceling Cancel Culture

1. Barack Obama, interviewed by Yara Shahidi and Obama Foundation program participants at the Obama Foundation Summit, October 29, 2019, Chicago, IL.

2. Ruth Bader Ginsburg, "Justice Ruth Bader Ginsburg Eulogy at Justice Scalia Memorial Service (C-SPAN)," streamed live on March 1, 2016, YouTube video, https://www.youtube.com/watch?v=jb_2GgE564A.

Part 3 Cultivating Moral Courage

1. StudyLight.org, accessed March 2, 2021, https://www.studylight.org/lexicons/greek/1342.html.

2. Lou Whitaker, "How Does Thinking Positive Thoughts Affect Neuroplasticity?," Meteor Education, accessed February 24, 2021, https://meteoreducation.com/how-does-thinking-positive-thoughts-affect-neuroplasticity/.

3. Shane Claiborne and Jonathan Wilson-Hartgrove, *Common Prayer Pocket Edition: A Liturgy for Ordinary Radicals* (Grand Rapids: Zondervan, 2012), 58.

Part 5 Where Did All the Glitter Go?

1. "Skin-to-Skin Contact," UNICEF, accessed February 25, 2021, https://www.unicef.org.uk/babyfriendly/baby-friendly-resources/implementing-standards-resources/skin-to-skin-contact/.

2. "Newborn Senses," University of Rochester Medical Center, accessed February 25, 2021, https://www.urmc.rochester.edu/encyclopedia/content.aspx?contenttypeid=90&contentid=P02631.

3. Colleen Walsh, "What the Nose Knows," *Harvard Gazette*, February 27, 2020, https://news.harvard.edu/gazette/story/2020/02/how-scent-emotion-and-memory-are-intertwined-and-exploited/.

4. Ken Wytsma, *Create vs. Copy: Embrace Change. Ignite Creativity. Break Through with Imagination* (Chicago: Moody, 2016), 32 (italics in the original).

Alexandra Kuykendall spends her days driving to multiple schools, figuring out what to feed her people, and searching for a better solution to the laundry dilemma. Author of *Loving My Actual Neighbor, Loving My Actual Life, Loving My Actual Christmas,* and *The Artist's Daughter,* Alex is co-hostess of *The Open Door Sisterhood* podcast. A trusted voice for today's Christian women, she speaks around the world on issues of parenting, faith, and identity. She lives in the shadows of downtown Denver with her husband, Derek, and their four daughters. Alex serves as the national network director for Project 1.27, a ministry that inspires, recruits, and provides resources to churches and families to foster and adopt the kids in their own backyard. You can connect with her at AlexandraKuykendall.com.

ALSO AVAILABLE FROM

Alexandra Kuykendall

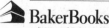

CONNECT WITH

ALEXANDRAKUYKENDALL.COM

Alex_Kuykendall

AlexandraKuykendall.Author

AlexandraKuykendall

TheOpenDoorSisterhood.com

LIKE THIS
BOOK?
Consider sharing it with others!

- Share or mention the book on your social media platforms. Use the hashtag **#SeekingOutGoodness**.

- Write a book review on your blog or on a retailer site.

- Pick up a copy for friends, family, or strangers— anyone who you think would enjoy and be challenged by its message!

- Recommend this book for your church, workplace, book club, or class.

- Follow Baker Books and Alexandra Kuykendall on social media and tell us what you like about the book.

f ReadBakerBooks	**f**	AlexandraKuykendall.Author
𝕏 ReadBakerBooks	**𝕏**	Alex_Kuykendall
◉ ReadBakerBooks	**◉**	AlexandraKuykendall